THE CRYSTAL CHALICE

WITH CONTRIBUTIONS BY:

Hayat Abuza
Jalelah Fraley
Pir Vilayat Inayat Khan
Saphira Barbara Linden
Elizabeth Rechtschaffen
Margaret Smith

the Crystal Chalice

Spiritual Themes for Women

Taj Inayat

Sufi Order Publications

NEW LEBANON, NEW YORK

1978

The Crystal Chalice
© 1978 by Sufi Order. All rights reserved

SUFI ORDER PUBLICATIONS
P.O. Box 396
New Lebanon, New York 12125

Printed in the United States of America
ISBN 0-930872-08-8

To
The Veiled One

The Inspiration of my inspiration

Contents

MEDITATION (continued)

DAILY LIFE

ACKNOWLEDGMENTS

The author extends heartfelt gratitude to Abadi Goodman and Hayat Abuza for their help in preparing the manuscript; to Barkat Curtin, who designed the cover and did some of the illustrations; and to Quan Yin for assistance in layout.

The following portions are reprinted by permission of their publishers:

pp. 10-12 from *The Silver Jubilee Souvenir of Mother Krishnabai's Renunciation*. Kanhangad, South India: Anandashram P.O. 670531, 1955.

pp. 17-21 from *Rabia, the Mystic, A.D. 717-801, and Her Fellow Saints of Islam*, Margaret Smith. London: Cambridge University Press, 1928.

pp. 30-31 from *New Seeds of Contemplation*, Thomas Merton. Abbey of Gethsemani, Inc., New Directions Publishing Corporation, 1961.

pp. 40-41 from *Something Beautiful for God*, Malcolm Muggeridge. Scranton: Ballantine, 1971.

pp. 80-81 from *Twenty Jataka Tales*, retold by Noor Inayat Khan. The Hague: East-West Publications Fonds bv, 1975.

ILLUSTRATIONS

All beauty is veiled by nature,
and the greater the beauty the more it is covered.
[Hazrat Inayat Khan]

THE CRYSTAL CHALICE

Introduction

This book has been compiled as a response to the plea of many spiritually oriented women who have not found the answer to their questions in traditional esoteric schools. Many schools do not always take into account the feminine nature of the seeker or the modern cultural context in which she functions. It is difficult also to find illuminated women who function as wife, mother, or career women. Until recently most spiritual models for women have emerged from Christian or Buddhist monastic life or from the celibate renunciate lives of the Hindus, but today as the West stops turning to the East for its spiritual values and recognizes the value of spirituality in everyday life, women are also looking for models who live right in the world while still maintaining a spiritual ideal.

In this age of uniformity the mystery that has enshrouded womanhood for ages is now being exposed and analyzed. Women themselves are removing the veils, wishing to step forward without the protection and limitation afforded by the customs and attitudes of the past. But the veiled aspect of womanhood now so readily discarded may prove to be a fundamental aspect of femininity. Historically woman's lack of outer power and activity has been the cause of her exploitation, but

1

on the other hand, these same qualities have allowed her to be empty of self and reach the heights of spiritual experience. Woman's true nature, and therefore her power, rises from the depth and is not readily apparent. She is often unable to express this depth without betraying her essence, just as words and thoughts, the very forms of expression of the spirit, often falsify expression by their superficiality and limitation.

Many women today object to this kind of interpretation of womanhood and strive to emulate the masculine values that have been the foundation of the Western technological world. Because of a lack of respectable models, women lack faith in their innate female nature. This combined with a highly developed ability to reflect contemporary trends has contributed to the sad spiritual state of women today. Yet the mistakes of the past are often the steppingstones to higher realizations. Some women, not finding fulfillment in exercising overt power, or at least sensing that this power has come with too great a price, are coming to see that real fulfillment lies in discovering and expressing one's real nature.

This discovery has broader dimensions: if we believe that the universe is one whole organism, then what is happening on one level is significant on all levels. We can look at woman's search for her soul as the earth's stirring in its sleep. The Persian mystical poet Jelaluddin Rumi expresses the idea of awakening very beautifully:

> *I died as mineral and became a plant,*
> *I died as plant and rose to animal,*
> *I died as animal and I was Man.*
> *Why should I fear? When was I less by dying?*
> *Yet once more I shall die as Man, to soar*
> *With angels blest; but even from angelhood I must pass on:*
> *All except God doth perish.*

Hazrat Inayat Khan, the great Sufi master, describes the present stage of the planet's evolution as "the awakening of

the consciousness of humanity to the divinity of man(kind)"[1]
Woman is called upon to fulfill a great role in this awakening
process. By accepting her femininity she can guide the thinking of the planet to value receptivity. Only through receptive
attunement to inner guidance can the next stage of planetary
evolution occur.

Ancient esotericism is expressed through what have
been termed the minor and major mysteries. The minor
mysteries, symbolized by the crescent moon, prepare the
initiate for transformation through purification and surrender.
Alchemically speaking, the transient is separated from the
eternal, and the individual self or perspective is crucified.

St. John the Baptist, the forerunner of Jesus, said,
"Prepare ye the way for the coming of the Lord . . . Make
straight the way." This is a call to cleanse the body, mind, and
heart. Physically we promote good health in order to provide
a suitable temple for the spirit; mentally we rid the mind of
negative thoughts, all judgments, and limitations in understanding; emotionally we rise above the personal perspective
and open the heart to the vastness of the universe and the
condition of humanity. The ultimate aim is always purification
of the individual self so that the consciousness of the One
Whole may emerge.

Woman epitomizes this state of pure readiness to receive,
symbolized by the moon which produces no light of its own but
shines with reflected light. In the major mysteries, the sun
symbolic of the Light of God (the Christ consciousness) dawns
from within the purified heart. The earth is presently engaged
in deep spiritual transformation. Learning the art of the moon
will prepare the planet for the dawning of the sun. Conscious

---

[1] *The Sufi Message*, 12 vols. (London: Barrie & Jenkins, 1967).
Subsequent quotations are from these volumes unless noted
otherwise.

unity with the divine perfection, emerging as a reality collectively and individually, makes possible the heralded new age.

The challenge of the new age woman is to find her true nature amidst a world which denies its value. With the power of compassion she will draw beings to a higher realization through her intuition and insight. Woman has a choice: she can continue to use her inborn attractiveness (which has been programmed into the genes of the human race by the Planner to ensure that the race will continue) as a means of serving her vanity and her individual ego, or she can use the charm of her purity and compassion to draw all beings into the realization of spiritual values. The latter is the art of conscious womanhood which alone can save mankind because she becomes the instrument of the transfiguration of the planet. Which will she choose? How can she become that which she wishes to become?

This understanding of the higher dimensions of womanhood can only be communicated from the depth, from heart to heart; most often in the silence or in a sigh. Few men would ever understand. I do not wish to imply that this knowledge is superior but that it is unique. The means of its transmission is affected by its sacred nature and therefore it is not abundant in the spiritual marketplace today. Unutterable is the knowledge of the wounded and resurrected heart, the heart which has become the living Holy Grail, the crystal chalice.

The information in this book is a tiny part of a vast awareness hidden in the depth of woman. It is a collection of essays and recollections, material that evolved out of women's meditation groups and suggestions and seed thoughts to help open woman's awareness of her inner being. Some things are very personal. Please take what is useful and disregard what is not. My hope is that something in these pages will ignite a spark or touch a chord in your being which will resonate with the Divine Presence.

WOMEN SAINTS

Women Absorbed in Divinity

Tradition is rich with accounts of the lives of the saints, yet many other holy women have lived, fulfilled their destiny, and died, unknown by the world and reachable only through the spirit. Stories and narratives of mystical women's lives are available but do not necessarily serve as access to the spiritual presence of their beings, which happens only when we are deeply moved by some aspect of their life or personality.

The following women, each uniquely manifesting an attribute of womanhood, have all touched me profoundly. At times my consciousness was altered under their influence and my love expanded to accommodate their divine love; sometimes their presence lighted my steps while I was passing through the dark valleys in life. They always inspired me to discover a deeper aspect of myself, the divine perfection dwelling within.

These few glimpses into saintly lives are intended to serve only as an opening to a deeper and more thorough research and to inspire communion with women motivated by a spiritual ideal who had to overcome many tests and trials preceding their union with God. Let them be an example when we are discouraged or weary with our little concerns and complaints. They can reach us beyond the walls of time and space, speaking to us from within, holding high the light upon our path, giving us that extra impetus which supplements our own strivings. Their grace awaits us.

These portraits are not meant to give detailed historical information. The included bibliography can put you in touch with richer knowledge of their lives.

MOTHER KRISHNABAI

Mother Krishnabai

Krishnabai was the second of six children, born at Haliyal in South India. Because of an inauspicious planetary configuration at the time of her birth, September 20, 1903, astrologers advised her parents to give her away. Not wishing to do so, they performed a ceremony of passing her back and forth to another person, under the stomach of a cow, in order to make ineffective the malevolent planetary influence.

A significant moment in her life was her father's death in 1914 which caused her deep sadness. She married in 1918, and gave birth to two sons in 1919 and 1921. When she was pregnant with her third child, her husband died suddenly in 1923, creating a void in her life. The third child, a daughter, died one month after birth.

Intent on preserving her chastity, she decided to die "in the time of her husband," and within a year of his death, she tried to end her life by swallowing opium. However her son, who normally slept very soundly, woke that night calling, "Where has my mother gone?" Soon the household was awakened, an emetic given, and her life saved.

Still grieved she tried to attain peace. She visited saints, did *japa* (recited mantra), and made offerings to deities. In 1923 she was taken by friends to the ashram of Swami Papa-Ramdas. As she approached the ashram she felt the union of a child returning to its mother. She took initiation

9

and began to unfold spiritually under Papa's guidance. After her return home she underwent great persecutions and tests. She wrote Papa that she wished to give up her householder position, come to the ashram, and spend her nights on the hills, working as a scavenger or sweeper for her food. She told her children they could come along and share her life, but they chose to remain in school and be taken care of by friends.

Walking to the ashram in pitch blackness, she wondered how she would find her way, when a light shone out of her feet guiding her along the path. When she arrived, Papa sent her a note: "Mother, you have come to your own home." When she stayed, some left because of the slander that was started. Soon she attained spiritual illumination. At Anandashram, she served Papa and the devotees, cooked, managed celebrations, supervised building projects, and toured with Papa around the world. Now, years after Papa's death, she oversees the ashram and gives blessings to all who come for spiritual nourishment.

Two excerpts from *The Silver Jubilee Souvenir of Mother Krishnabai's Renunciation* give examples of Mother Krishnabai's service and the influence of her atmosphere on those around her:

> The first time that I met Mataji was during the world tour of Swami Ramdas and his party. During their short sojourn in England, I was privileged to drive them around the country on their visits to the various religious societies and meetings.
>
> Mataji, although always present on these excursions, was rarely noticed by most people, so successful was she in keeping herself in the background, out of the limelight. Although silent and unobtrusive, she spent all her time furnishing the needs of the party and she spared neither energy nor comfort. This is just one of the admirable qualities that endear her to all with whom she comes into contact.
>
> This constant desire to serve without reward or gratitude is a perfect living example of Christ's words: "Do not give your

alms in public places!'' To us who were not used to it, it was a striking example of selfless sacrifice. Her ever-present smile and the atmosphere of divine love that surrounded her served to present a minute part of the personality of the Holy Mother. Although the tour presented great hardships to her, she was ever ready and ever cheerful to serve Papa.

I did not see Mataji after those blissful two weeks. It was only after coming to Anandashram that the picture was enlarged. It is the constant care, love, and guiding force of the Mother that keeps the Ashram working smoothly as one unit. Those who have visited it know what a monumental task this is for one person. Whenever there is some difficulty to overcome, some problem to be worked out, or some need to be fulfilled, Mataji always appears on the scene from nowhere, as though drawn by the presence of human needs. She seems to know the needs of every person that enters the gates and she quietly sees to it that they are met. If any request is made to her, she willingly gives all she has with no thought of the morrow. In her efforts to be of service she is unstinting and untiring.

Only after looking into those eyes so filled with love, turned equally on prince and pauper or saint and sinner, can one possibly begin to know how divine is the being of Mataji. She is truly a living personification of divine love and service. When one sees Papa and Mataji together, one can clearly see in this duality the divine unity, or what we term as Father-Mother. God is one, so are Mataji and Ramdas one. Trying to confine Mataji to a few lines of poor prose is like trying to confine the ocean to a stream, or God to a name. (George A. Dudley, ''A Personification of Divine Love'')

Swami Satchidananda, who lives at Anandashram now, wrote of the experience of traveling with Mother Krishnabai and seeing life through her eyes:

Wherever you went, Mother, I found your heart was with the poor. You vehemently protested and argued with us when we said that all the people of the West had plenty. How we felt ashamed of our own narrowness of vision when you traced out the poor in the places we visited and helped them in whatever way you could. What a great joy it was to see how you showered your love on the English gardener of Jayaram House where we stayed in London. The old man was coming for work in the severe cold putting on a torn coat, a pair of worn out gloves that had seen at least half the winters he had seen, and a weathered hat. You saw him in that pitiable condition. Nobody else knew what he carried with him home in the heavy bag that you gave him, shall I say, stealthily!

Little did I know how clever you were in hiding your virtues. We are told, "What your right hand gives, your left hand would not know." How true this is in your case, Mother! When you were packing things on the eve of our departure from Bombay you took many extra new pieces of warm clothing like a woolen overcoat, shirts and so on. I asked you why we should carry items that we would never use, which would only increase the weight of the luggage. You slowly whispered into my ear, "There may be some poor people in Europe who would badly need these things. We shall give these garments away to them. Let us not mind the extra weight at present."

When we lived with our rich hosts in America in the midst of luxury, I could feel your heart bleeding for the poor and the destitute in India. You were then busy planning how and when to build a hut for some homeless workers of the ashram, how to find a job for S———, and how to keep the big families of G——— and M——— going. Whenever you gave me an inkling of what you thought, I remembered how Swami Vivekananda wept bitterly for the poor in India when he was in the midst of the plenty of America. (Swami Satchidananda, "With Mataji Abroad")

Six years ago I was struck with an intense desire to visit Mother Krishnabai, who is called Mataji. I had known of her through books, all praising her as one of India's greatest living saints. At the time, it didn't seem feasible for me to go to India because my younger child was only a few months old. However, the desire to meet this saint cleared every obstacle and soon circumstances permitted me to travel to India with my baby who also received her *darshan* (holy glance) and blessing.

When we arrived she was extremely ill and only able to sit up occasionally. Once a day she walked a short distance to the bhajan hall to sing Ram Nam with the devotees of Papa Ramdas. During this last occasion a great blessing was bestowed upon me and her divinity was radiantly revealed. She walked so slowly to her chair; she was tiny, weighing perhaps only eighty pounds.

She looked up at a picture of Papa Ramdas, her guru and spiritual partner. The expression on her face will live within me as one of the strongest impressions of my life. It was clear that she was not worshipping the personality or form of Papa, but that it served as a means of contact with the transcendent, all-pervading divine Presence. While she was lost in contemplation two traveling *sadhus* were ushered into her presence. When they bowed before her feet, she bowed in return, and I perceived that she saw the same all-pervading divine Presence in them. She invited them to go to the kitchen for food. Then she bowed before the picture of Papa and returned to her room.

She had shared so much with me without ever saying a word or even acknowledging my presence. Her silent but direct message to me was: "Don't look at me, look at what I'm looking at." She changed my life by teaching me not to cling to her image, but to do as she does: become as nothing before the Lord.

OM SRI RAM JAI RAM JAI JAI RAM

HAZRAT BABAJAN

Hazrat Babajan

A native of Baluchistan (between Afghanistan and India), Hazrat Babajan traveled to India and settled in Poona under a neem tree around 1900. Her powerful presence attracted many, Hindus and Muslims alike.

The scanty facts about this remarkable woman's life do not reflect the deep effect Hazrat Babajan had upon my life and personality. I would call her my "fairy godmother" in some sense, but don't be deceived by this term, for her wand is like a red-hot branding iron, stamping one with the vision of God. I include her in these glimpses of spiritual women because of several personal inner encounters with her. Her spirit can be reached, but only if you are prepared to pass through the test of fire.

Travelling on the mystical path, one encounters beings who have a shattering effect upon our ego-sense, that image that we believe ourselves to be. Sometimes their effect is so devastating to our sense of limitation that during the time they thrust the power of their realization upon our soul, we stand illuminated by the light of God that shines through them.

Such a being is the woman dervish Hazrat Babajan, whom pilgrims pass by on the way to their heart's fulfillment. Not only does the Sufi pass by the glare of her scrutiny on the inner planes, but some have passed by her on the earth plane and received her blessing here. This wizened and haggard figure, by kissing Meher Baba on the forehead, catapulted him into spiritual life. I feel it was this same woman who beckoned Hazrat Inayat Khan to eat food from her mouth, thus bestowing upon him a spiritual blessing.

Her face is chiseled by age, suffering, and annihilation, for she wishes only God to live in her. She gives you food from her mouth; you must be prepared to accept that which is despicable and holy: despicable from the point of view of the world and holy because it is made holy by consciousness of the divine Presence. If you come to her you cannot fear annihilation, otherwise you will regret having gone close to destruction. One will never receive less than the truth from her, and she can smite you out of love.

She says in her dervish way: "I am the wishing well. Yes, I wish you well. All is well that is wished by God. Do you wish God well? Well then, carry out His wish. Throw a *paisa* (penny) in the well and in a million years it turns to gold. That's doing without reward and wishing for someone else. If you wish for God, I will come to you."

Rabia

MARGARET SMITH

Rabia al-Adawiyya al-Qaysiyya of Basra represents one of the most outstanding personalities in the history of Sufism. Born into a poor home, about A.D. 713, the fourth (*rabia*) daughter, she was stolen as a child and sold into slavery, but the sanctity of her character and the evident signs of divine grace given to her so impressed her master that he set her free, in order that she might give herself to the service of a greater Master.

She retired to a life of seclusion, at first in the desert outside the city, and then in Basra itself. She remained unmarried and gathered around her many disciples and associates who came to seek her counsel or her prayers or listen to her teaching. Her devotion to her Lord and Master never seems to have led her to disassociate herself from her fellow-beings, except for the purpose of communing with the One, Who had the first claim upon her service and her time.

Unlike most of the great Sufis, she had no *shaykh* or teacher and little access to literature. While the majority of the Sufis of this early period were ascetics or quietists, she was a true mystic, marked by a glowing exaltation which places her among the great mystics of all time. Her teaching marks the

Margaret Smith was a Fellow of Girton College, Cambridge, England.

end of the early ascetic school of Sufism and a new conception of the human soul's relationship with the Divine which, while based nominally upon the Qur'an and the traditions, actually has little in common with the dogmatic teachings of orthodox Islam.

Rabia's disciples and associates included the most famous theologians and mystics of her time, and her biographers associate her with the great Sufi ascetic and preacher Hasan of Basra, although she could have known him only in his old age, while she herself was still a young girl. It is related that when his friends and disciples were gathered together to listen to him, if Rabia al-Adawiyya was not present in the assembly, he refused to address them. When asked why, when so many rich and distinguished folk were there to hear him, he should refuse to give an address because one poor woman was absent, he replied: "The potion prepared for an elephant cannot be poured down the throat of ants." This shows the great reverence and respect with which Rabia was regarded by those who knew her. It is said that this power of attraction extended even to animals and that such wild and timid creatures as deer, gazelle, and mountain goats would gather round her without fear.

Rabia's life was one of extreme simplicity and other-worldliness and, although she was frequently offered alleviations for her poverty and exhorted to seek help for herself from her wealthy friends, she steadfastly refused to do so, saying, "Will God forget the poor because of their poverty or remember the rich because of their riches? Since He knows my state, what have I to remind Him of? What He wills, we should also will."

She died at Basra in A.D. 801, in the sure faith that she was passing into the Presence of her Lord. She bade those around her to go out to leave the way clear for the coming of His messengers, and as they went out, they believed that they heard a voice saying, "O soul at rest, return unto thy Lord, satisfied with Him, giving satisfaction to Him. So enter among My servants, into My Paradise." After her death she was seen in a dream and asked how she had escaped from Munkar and Nakir, the two angels of death, when they asked her, "Who is thy Lord?" She replied, "I said, 'Return and tell your Lord: notwithstanding the thousands upon thousands of Thy creatures Thou has not forgotten a weak old woman. I, who had only Thee in all the world, have never forgotten Thee, that Thou shouldst ask, who is thy Lord?' "

Rabia's sense of the infinite greatness and majesty of God, and the infinite littleness of His creatures in comparison with Him did not prevent her from believing in the possibility of the closest and tenderest relationship between the human soul and its Lord. Rabia had a deep sense of sin and its power to separate the soul from God; she taught the need for re-pentance; turning the back on the old life of self-will and self-indulgence and turning the face to the new life lived in accordance with the divine Will. "The fruit of wisdom," she said, "is to turn one's face towards God." Repentance she held to be a grace from the Giver of every good and perfect gift, offered for the acceptance of the willing seeker.

Rabia laid stress on the need not only for outward purification from vice and the grosser sins, but also for the purification of the inner self, so that the feelings, motives and will might be brought into harmony with the Eternal Will. To Rabia the path meant complete detachment from the claims of this world and the lower self with much time given to seclusion, solitude, and contemplation. To Rabia God was chiefly the Friend and the Beloved, the joy and desire of her soul, with Whom she lived in closest intimacy, conscious always of His Presence and His unfailing help, and in Whom she felt that she lived and moved and had her being. At night, when she retired to sleep upon her roof, she used to pray, "O my Lord, the stars are shining, and the eyes of man are closed, and the kings have shut their doors, and every lover is alone with his beloved, and here am I, alone with Thee.''

The love of God, she taught, must be an all-absorbing love, so that it obliterated not only all false loves, but all hatred too. Asked whether she held Satan as an enemy, she replied, ''My love for God leaves no room for hating Satan.'' She took fire in one hand and water in the other saying, ''I am going to light a fire in Paradise and pour water on the flames of Hell, so that both veils may be taken away from those who are journeying towards God and they may look toward their Lord without any object of hope or motive of fear. I have not served God from fear of Hell, for I should be a wretched hireling if I did it from fear. Nor have I served Him from love of Paradise, for I should be an unworthy servant if I did it in hope of reward; but I have served Him only for the love of Him and desire for Him.''

WORDS OF RABIA

In two ways have I loved Thee, selfishly
And with a love that worthy is of Thee.
In selfish love my joy in Thee I find,
While to all else, and others, I am blind.
But in that love which seeks Thee worthily,
The veil is raised, that I may look on Thee.
Yet is the praise in that or this, not mine;
In this and that, the praise is wholly Thine.

O my Lord, if I worship Thee from fear of Hell, consume me therein, and if I worship Thee in hope of Paradise, exclude me thence; but if I worship Thee for Thine own sake, then withhold not from me Thine Eternal Beauty.

The groaning and the yearning of the love of God will not be satisfied until it is satisfied in the Beloved.

My heart, Beloved, is Thy dwelling-place.
While others seek my body's company,
My body treats its guests with friendliness,
But, for my soul, I seek no guest but Thee.

I have ceased to exist and have passed out of self: I have become one with God and am altogether His.

My peace I find within that solitude
Wherein I dwell alone with my Beloved,
The Immortal Lover, for Whose sake I cast
Aside all mortal loves. To Him, the One
And only Fair, All-Beautiful, I turn
My face, in contemplation, seeking thus
The satisfaction of my soul's desire.
From Him it came, to Him it turns again,
And finds in Him its everlasting joy
And life eternal: lost to self, but found
In Him, the One, the Real, for evermore.

Three Women and a Sage

This dialogue between three women in the spiritual hierarchy and a sage was an inspiration that came to Pir Vilayat and me while talking about current values of womanhood and wondering how the challenges that face women today would be looked at from the vantage point of these women, each so unique in her outlook on reality and womanhood. The women are Rabia al-Adawiyya, described as "that woman who lost herself in union with the Divine, that one accepted as a second spotless Mary," her atmosphere is holy and feminine; Hazrat Babajan, a fanatical woman dervish, uncompromising and sexless; Ma, a matronly, jovial, practical, imperturbable, large, loving, and manifestation-oriented woman. The sage is a divine man whose consciousness has become so vast as to accommodate all beings yet at the same time vibrate and react to every shade of human feeling.

Question. What is the teaching for women today?

Rabia. We women don't agree. Ma sees what I don't see and Hazrat Babajan doesn't see what I see. Women don't agree because they cover a larger gamut of values than the stars in the sky and because—

Hazrat Babajan [*interrupting*]. —because they can't express the depth of their being.

Ma [*laughing*]. You all make such mysteries of women, we have to get on with her problems. What are her problems? There's the mother who tries to possess her daughter (the son will probably rebel), the woman who's afraid of going out into the storm of life, the woman who tries to compete with man, and the woman who tries to hide her feelings because she doesn't know how to defend them when being challenged by man.

Rabia. Yes, true, But you've discounted the women who have a spiritual calling and must live in the world.

Hazrat Babajan. There's *no* compromise. You must follow your ideal and if it breaks up a marriage, so what? Marriage is the lower function—it was made for procreation.

Ma. No, it's to protect women against the thoughtlessness and ruthlessness of primitive men. Today women aren't protected as much because they wish to be free. They're doing away with their protection because they don't need it as much as they used to.

Rabia. I am wedded to God alone and I discovered very soon that I could not have two lovers. A woman can't have two lovers if she's really a woman. How is there room in one's heart for a human beloved if all one's heart is taken by God?

Ma. But this is not for all women. The Divine Beloved appears as the human beloved.

Hazrat Babajan. What a travesty! Most times the personal beloved hides the Divine Beloved instead of manifesting Him.

Ma. You have to make him. It's the job of woman to make her husband transparent to the divine. She is the real guru who gives birth to the spirituality of her husband.

Hazrat Babajan. —but his interests are often elsewhere.

Ma. It's a very great art. The greater the woman, the more she is able to kindle the light of spirituality in a man who is preoccupied with the world.

Rabia. Hallowed are those women whose husbands are naturally inclined towards the spiritual path. It's new because now the spiritual men respect the spiritual life of their women, whereas before they didn't like that competition or they admired it in silence.

Ma. You have to help women in their practical problems. They don't like generalizations. Take each problem in turn.

Rabia. But if you look into the problem, you'll lose sight of the spiritual significance.

Hazrat Babajan. You have to be ruthless in introducing the spiritual life, wherever it is—marriage or no marriage.

Ma. But not at the cost of human problems.

Hazrat Babajan. Yes! At the cost of human problems, because they are only subsidiary and people wallow in them. So they fail to see the spiritual values.

Rabia. You see, women can't agree. Women are capable of the greatest height of inspiration but on the other hand are capable of vegetating in a state of complacency. They seek for a settled condition where they're assured of a livelihood and security from problems so they can get on with their homekeeping.

Hazrat Babajan. Yes, but the woman who braves the storm of life, allowing herself to be annihilated, receives the greatest security: the divine Presence.

Rabia. But nature has made women seek security because it's for the male to go out and find prey to feed the young. The women have to insure the security of the home, and that has tended to make women settle themselves and remain in that state until someone makes them feel envious of men, who seem to have a more exciting life and a greater outlet for their unfoldment. Then women seek to compete with men; they develop qualities which are unfeminine. Life is changed now; duties of the home have decreased, so there is more scope for women to play a part beyond the home, in business, politics, etc.

Sage. Something new is happening in relationships. A woman should work with her husband or beloved in his work instead of seeking another boss, and the children should be cared for by the community. The special care of the mother is important but it's also good for the children to open up to the community and to other children. This inter-work relationship is only possible when the woman is able to be a co-worker. It means a completely new approach to marriage; the man marries someone who he feels can be his associate in work rather than a woman who will be able to look after the home. You may be surprised to hear me say this as it differs from by background in India, which had its beauty, but where I saw women suffering very much. They were the victims of a system organized to curb the activities of women, because many, if they had been given leeway, would have taken too many liberties, gotten hysterical, or broken down. The atmosphere becomes very lax and it takes the severity of the male to maintain a certain direction. That's why the education that has to be given to women is in holding themselves together, working with emotions—controlling them, lifting them, and watching them—familiarizing themselves with different emotions, and seeing where emotions take them. The world of emotion is much more developed in women than in men.

Hazrat Babajan. Yes, that's why women who are devoted to the God ideal have to overcome their womanhood.

Rabia. No, this is just the issue. Woman doesn't overcome her womanhood when she expresses herself as the bride of God.

Ma. No, when women are in life, they can't be the bride of God, but they can be the daughter of God. They must find a way of working with their husbands and finding the proper relationship with them so they may keep their femininity. Women don't have to perform the same spiritual role as men.

Sage. I introduced priesthood for women.

Hazrat Babajan. Yes, sometimes it is successful, but many women confuse spirituality with sentimentality unless they overcome their human emotions.

Rabia. No, they can sublimate their emotions. The task given to the leader of women is to teach women how to go through emotions and how to sublimate them.

Sage. Women's emotions are maintained in a certain balance by her relationship with men. Women themselves lose the handle on their emotions in the absence of coordination between their emotions and the emotions of men, because they're trying to compete instead of complete. So the solution is for women to work together with men in a very close relationship and for men and women to choose mates who can be co-workers. Women should know how to find a relationship with God, with the teacher, with husbands or lovers, with all other men, and with women. Women should be taught how to pray.

Rabia. Yes, women should be taught how to pray. Not in their human feelings, but how to reach that source of life that is immaculate and pray in that place, and then how to return into their human feelings again; how to open up their feeling to beings and how to veil themselves; how to maintain their own when challenged by a man without getting upset and agitated; how to overcome the natural tendency of women to be rivals by channeling their emotions into collective group consciousness; how to confide in one another without idle gossip; how to keep a secret; how to check themselves from talking about things that they should hold in their heart; and how to deal with children.

Sage. Women should be able to correct children without getting angry. On the other hand, nature gave even anger as a tool and there are times when the semblance of anger is the only thing that will control the child. But it is also important for women to develop the detachment that Hazrat Babajan is talking about. Women must learn to master emotion, to go from strong emotion to non-emotion. You see how each of these three women has her own emotion.

Ma. No, we have a whole gamut of emotions. It's just that one of us is oriented in one direction and one in another.

Hazrat Babajan. I don't understand all this talk about emotion; it's human weakness. Why does one want to wallow in the inferior netherworlds when there's divine Perfection to be experienced by every soul, man or woman—it just doesn't make any difference.

Sage. She is lost in her path and she has found herself in her path. Everyone has a path and yet there is a place where the paths meet and it is in the consciousness of God. Let women find their own individual paths and let them also try to meet at the place where the paths meet.

There are three kinds of virgins. One, commonly considered a virgin, who has never had association with a man; another is the virgin in heart, whose love is centered in one beloved only; and the third is the virgin in soul, who considers man as God. She alone can give birth to a divine child.

[*Hazrat Inayat Khan*]

Mary, Mother of Jesus

It is difficult for me to write about Mary in a meaningful way other than from personal mystical experience. I view reality as a total Being containing many sub-beings, not fractions within itself, but stages of awakening within, just as the seed is a state of the flower as yet unfolded rather than a segment or fraction of it. Therefore beings cannot be really connected to one another in a relationship of "you and I" but only "I and i" or

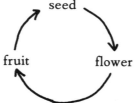

In this form of relationship, beyond, but deep within, I write about Mary.

Entering into the Virgin Mary's consciousness is entering into the Christ Spirit in humanity. She was the pure chalice capable of bearing divinity in creation. Purity here not only implies free from sin, but free from self.

Through her love for Jesus, she did not wish to be spared from his trial. She descended into the agony of human suffering, which was embodied in her son's crucifixion, and with a broken heart she was lost in the sea of his blood. As she shared the agony of Jesus, she also participated fully in his resurrection. She was crowned in heaven with the consciousness of divine Perfection, above all duality of good and evil or joy and pain, thus attaining Supreme Union.

In the actual living, human person who is the Virgin Mother of Christ are all the poverty and all the wisdom of all the saints. It all came to them through her, and is in her. The sanctity of all the saints is a participation in her sanctity, because in the order He has established God wills that all graces come to men through Mary.

That is why to love her and to know her is to discover the true meaning of everything and to have access to all wisdom. Without her, the knowledge of Christ is only speculation. But in her it becomes experience because all the humility and poverty, without which Christ cannot be known, were given to her. Her sanctity is the silence in which alone Christ can be heard, and the voice of God becomes an experience to us through her contemplation . . . .

Mary's chief glory is in her nothingness, in being the *"handmaid* of the Lord,'' as one who is becoming the Mother of God acted simply in loving submission to His command, in the pure obedience of faith. She is blessed not because of some mythical pseudo-divine prerogative, but in all her human and womanly limitations as *one who has believed.* It is the faith and the fidelity of this humble handmaid, "full of grace,'' that enable her to be the perfect instrument of God, and nothing else but His instrument. The work that was done in her was purely the work of God. "He that is mighty hath done great things in me.'' The glory of Mary is purely and simply the glory of God in her, and she, like anyone else, can say that she has nothing that she has not received from Him through Christ.

As a matter of fact, this is precisely her greatest glory: that having nothing of her own, retaining nothing of a "self'' that could glory in anything for her own sake, she placed no obstacle to the mercy of God and in no way resisted His love and His will. Hence she received *more* from Him than any other saint. He was able to accomplish His will perfectly in her, and His liberty was in no way hindered or turned from its purpose by the presence of an egotistical self in Mary. She was and is in the highest sense a person precisely because, being "immaculate," she was free from every taint of selfishness that might obscure God's light in her being. She was then a freedom that obeyed Him perfectly and in this obedience found the fulfillment of perfect love. (Thomas Merton, *New Seeds of Contemplation*)

The Broken Heart

More than any other saint, Mary embodies the meaning of the broken heart; her example can guide sensitive persons through this experience in their own lives. There is a stage in the awakening of God through humanity in which He experiences His crucifixion. This experience of God is felt by human beings when they experience cosmic suffering on earth. It is the initiation of the broken heart: the moment when one wishes to take upon oneself the broken heart of God. For "out of the shell of the broken heart emerges the newborn soul," and this newborn soul is God's being.

First one realizes that the Only Being has left the solitude of abstraction and unity to become a physical reality: the purpose of creation and the condition for resurrection. The seed becomes the plant which means the Only Being has literally become humanity; humanity is a stage in the unfoldment of God's Being. If this is fully experienced it is very sobering, and indeed if one feels the depth of the condition of God in humanity, it makes one's heart bleed because one sees how things could be. It is like mud on the snow or a beautiful thing that is broken.

This is the act of Christ on the cross: to become the world, to accept the condition of the Beloved, whose hands and feet are nailed and who has delivered Himself out of love as a gift to those who betray Him. The heart of God goes through such agony after having given Himself to those very people who make Him go through agony.

Do we really know what it means to deliver ourselves out of love? It means *total* giving, not giving part and holding part back. It is not giving oneself in expectation or even hope of return, such as recognition, spiritual realization, or life hereafter in heaven. It is loving so much that the outcome is irrelevant: life or death, sinking or swimming, poison or nectar.

This is the condition of God. He has given His being, perfect and unlimited, out of love into the fragments of Himself (creatures) that they (we) may enjoy the perfection that He Himself experiences. Then He is betrayed by these very beings. So when Christ said, ''Why has Thou abandoned me?'' He was speaking from the divine consciousness saying, ''Why has thou (creatures) abandoned Me (God)?'' This is the experience of cosmic suffering because it is God who is suffering.

Do we wish to experience the condition of God? Is our love for the Beloved so strong that the Beloved's pain is our joy?

> *I would willingly die a thousand deaths if by dying I could attain Thy most lofty presence. If it were a cup of poison Thy beloved hand offered, I would prefer that poison to the bowl of nectar. I value the dust under Thy feet, my Precious One, most of all the treasures the earth holds. If my head could touch the earth of Thy dwelling-place, I would proudly refuse Khusru's crown. I would gladly sacrifice all pleasures the earth can offer me, if I could only retain Thy pain in my feeling heart.*

---

[1]*The Complete Sayings of Hazrat Inayat Khan*, (New Lebanon, New York: Sufi Order Publications, 1978).

Thus, the words of Christ become clear: "Take up the cross and follow Me."

How do we dare claim to be the followers of the prophet and to accept suffering, when we can't even accept the lack of understanding or the criticism of our fellow men. We complain when situations seem to go wrong from our point of view, when what we have been working for falls apart, or when our love is not returned. These are only small pin pricks to our ego and vanity, yet we recoil from them in daily life. We expect to have the love and understanding of others and are unwilling to accept the pain involved in loving, understanding, and accommodating "thorny" people in our own being.

Hazrat Inayat Khan says the *Murshid* (teacher) accepts the grit of sand and transforms it into a pearl (in his being). By accepting the thorns that life offers, we prepare ourselves to be "invited to share in the divine banquet, where the host offers us a cup of poison" ('al Hallaj). The acceptance of this cup of poison is the very act that constitutes resurrection. And imagine the joy when we at last realize that it was never meant that things should be perfect on the physical plane, but that a being, by trying to make them perfect, becomes divine!

Divine consciousness contains the realization of the purpose of creation, the purpose of life, the purpose of suffering and the answer to all the heart-felt questions that humans ponder when faced with the problems of life. The only condition that can heal a broken heart is peace, which comes in discovering that situations are "as they should be" and that despite appearances to the contrary, "all is well."

We could ask ourselves what goal could possibly be so great as to positively offset the extreme suffering humans have endured on earth: the horrors of the concentration camps, the slow agonizing disintegration of the body through disease, the psychic and physical torture applied to citizens by oppressive governments, or the loss of loved ones. But when consciousness is expanded to encompass the viewpoint of the Total Being, the ability to see perfection emerges out of the fiasco and peace is experienced. For by viewing from this vantage point, one sees that it is God who has limited Himself in humanity, it is God who suffers and it is God who emerges out of the shards of limitation to realize in each creature His perfection. It is the birth of God through humanity, made possible by God's gift of *free will*.

In order to appreciate the deeper harmonics of that precious pearl, "spiritual freedom," one has to pass through the Sufi initiation which is, as one ancient Sufi said, "The passing away of the merely human into the sheer divine." For only in viewing from the perspective of Unity Consciousness can the full scope of divine freedom be realized, just as after a spring shower the glory of the earth radiantly emerges out of the staleness of what was.

Divine freedom is God's own attainment (resurrection) through bearing the cross of matter and giving Himself lovingly but precariously into the hands of man. By refusing to bow down before the image of man—Adam—the archangel Lucifer expressed to God his fear of the hazard He would incur through the process of incarnation. As a result, Lucifer has had to carry the stigma of his denial throughout history (although in reality he has been reinstated to his former position). Yet God in His infinite wisdom (*Maarifah*) and infinite sacrifice (*Rahmaniyat*) wedded His spirit to creation in what is symbolized by the alchemical marriage.

Two crosses, or annihilations, are born from this marriage. One cross is from the point of view of man and the other from the point of view of God. The first is the crucifixion of man's ego. Of this cross, Hazrat Inayat Khan says, "This cross he (the spiritual aspirant) carries during his progress. It is the ugly passions, the love of comforts and satisfaction in anger and bitterness that he has to fight first; and when he has conquered these, the next trouble he has to meet is that still more subtle enemy of himself in his mind, the sensitivity to what others say, to the opinions of others about himself. He is anxious to know everybody's opinion about him, or what anybody says against him, or if his dignity or position is hurt in any way." Liberation from one's ego permits one to experience more and more freedom resulting in a more harmonious blending with all of creation. This is the resurrection from the "little cross."

The "great cross" is the annihilation the divine consciousness experiences, which is the crucifixion of the divine Ego. It is the original sacrifice of the state of Unity Consciousness into the state of humanity. It was of this act that 'al Hallaj spoke when he advised Bastami to give up isolation (*tajrid*) for union (*tawhid*). God's sacrifice is the sacrifice of His unity into man's state of duality, while man's sacrifice is that of his duality into God's unity.

Whereas Lucifer was unable to see the great Intention (*Ma'ana*) behind creation, God in His omniscience contemplated in anticipation the ultimate reinstation of His original unity through the resurrection that He was to undergo in each of the projections (creatures) of Himself. It is the resurrection from the "great cross" that is the formation of omega consciousness.

When a human being incorporates the divine view, he experiences this "great cross" as an upheaval in the deepest depths of his soul, as a cosmic earthquake that disintegrates the very foundations of existence. It is out of this devastation that the reborn Divine Being (the *Rassoul*) emerges in true freedom, dancing, soaring, unfolding the wings of consciousness, at last totally free. "And I saw a new heaven and a new earth, for the former heaven and former earth were passed away" (John, *Revelations*).

37

MOTHER TERESA

Mother Teresa

Mother Teresa was born in Yugoslavia in 1910 and entered into the Loreto Convent in Ireland in 1928, feeling that this path would lead her to fulfilling her deepest desire. From 1929-1948 she taught in a school in Calcutta and in 1946 she requested permission to work in the Calcutta slums. In 1948 she left the convent, donned a sari, took nurses training, and began her mission. In 1949 she began training sisters. Since then she has opened missionary centers in Rome, Venezuela, Ceylon, Australia, and Jordan. In 1971 she was awarded the Pope John XXIII Peace Prize presented by Pope Paul VI and in 1971 the Kenny International Award for Outstanding Services for Mankind.

By now, the extraordinary being of Mother Teresa has become known to the world, bringing the message of selfless love and service as a beacon of hope shining in these dark hours. Millions of people have been touched by her without ever having met her, only through hearing of the work she and her sisters have been doing in India for nearly thirty years. Mother Teresa and her sisters make daily rounds of Calcutta, picking up the dying and wretched from the streets, rescuing tiny newborns from the rubbish heaps, and nursing the lepers and hospital rejects. All is a sacrament, for she sees in each being the body of Christ. She wishes every person to have, at least in their dying moment, the experience of being loved and cared for. She and the sisters become the channel for God's concern.

She herself does not wish praise or fame, but wishes the plight of the poor and needy throughout the world to be noticed and healed so that these people can be given the dignity of life and love that is their human birthright as the beloved ones of God. People who have met her speak with unabashed fervor:

Doing something beautiful for God is, for Mother Teresa, what life is about. Everything, in that it is for God, becomes beautiful, whatever it may be; as does every human soul participating in this purpose, whoever he or she may be. In manifesting this, in themselves and in their lives and work, Mother Teresa and the Missionaries of Charity provide a living witness to the power and truth of what Jesus came to proclaim. His light shines in them. When I think of them in Calcutta, as I often do, it is not the bare house in a dark slum that is conjured up in my mind, but a light shining and a joy abounding. I see them diligently and cheerfully constructing something beautiful for God out of the human misery and affliction that lies around them. One of their leper settlements is near a slaughter-house whose stench in the ordinary way might easily make me retch. There, with Mother Teresa, I scarcely noticed it; another fragrance had swallowed it up.

For those of us who find difficulty in grasping with our minds Christ's great propositions of love which make such dedication possible, someone like Mother Teresa is a godsend. She is this love in person; through her, we can reach it, and hold it, and incorporate it in ourselves. Everyone feels this. I was watching recently the faces of people as they listened to her— just ordinary people who had crowded into a school hall to hear her. Every face, young and old, simple and sophisticated, was rapt, hanging on her words; not because of the words themselves —they were ordinary enough—but because of her. Some quality that came across over and above the words held their attention.

A luminosity seemed to fill the school hall, illumining the rapt faces, penetrating into every mind and heart.

When she had finished and the meeting was over, they all wanted to touch her hand; to be physically near her for a moment; to partake of her, as it were. She looked so small and frail and tired standing there, giving herself. Yet this, I reflected, is how we may find salvation. Giving, not receiving; the anti-ad, the dispensing rather than the consuming society; dying in order to live. One old man, not content just to take her hand, bent his grey head down to kiss it. So they do to queens and eminences and great seigniors. In this particular case, it was a gesture of perfect thankfulness to God—in which I shared—for helping our poor stumbling minds and fearful hearts by showing us his everlasting truth in the guise of one homely face going about His work of love. (Malcolm Muggeridge, *Something Beautiful for God*)

And another personal account:

In October, 1975, the United Nations General Assembly on the occasion of its 30th Anniversary was addressed by leading figures of the world's religions. Mother Teresa was there. She sat on a chair, her feet barely touching the ground, her gnarled hands folded in her lap. Such a tiny lady, wrapped in a white sari with blue trim, warmed by an ancient grey sweater, everything about her was so utterly simple. When her turn came to speak, she walked to the podium, barely reached the microphone, and said:

"Are we ready to love? Are we ready to love to the point of pain, as Jesus Christ has taught us? Until we are ready to love, neither the United Nations nor all the governments and agencies in the world can do anything to help the poor and the starving. In the Bible we read, 'I was hungry and you did not feed me, I was homeless and you did not give me shelter, I was naked and you did not clothe me.' The poor people in our world need our help, but we do not know them. If we knew them, we would love them, as Jesus Christ taught us to love. We have to learn to love to the point of pain."

Many eyes filled with tears, a quiet hush embraced the Truth. Mother then asked to be allowed to greet everyone

41

present, including those who were upstairs watching the proceedings on closed-circuit television. The speakers all joined this little procession, and everyone exchanged greetings on that momentous morning. When she took my hands into hers, looking into my eyes to convey the blessing of God, the streaming tears were lit by joy, "and that joy no man taketh away."

Afterwards, we visited one of her two New York City centers. (Her order is called the Missionaries of Charity with centers throughout Europe, the Americas and Australia, as well as in India.) The order includes a lay order of housewives and their families; ordinary people do much of the work. Mother says that the greatest poverty in the West is loneliness, so much of the work in the West includes visiting the sick, the old, and those in hospitals. They emphasize tangible work such as alcoholic rehabilitation, drug counseling, feeding programs, children's after-school education, and guitar masses in prisons.

The cosmic dimension of their work is that everything one would wish to do for the Christ, one does for one's fellow men in whom He is reflected. Her sisters are the most glowing and joyous ladies we had ever met, their love delighting all who come in contact with them. Mother Teresa visits most of her centers from time to time, and on one such visit we went to hear her again, and she started by saying, "Are we ready to love? Are we ready to love to the point of pain?" (Iman Ibranyi-Kiss, unpublished)

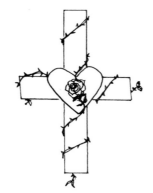

WORDS OF MOTHER TERESA

Faith is a gift of God. Without it there would be no life. And our work, to be fruitful and to be all for God, and beautiful, has to be built on faith. Faith in Christ who said, "I was hungry, I was naked, I was sick, and I was homeless and you did that to me." On these words of His all our work is based.

ON PRAYER

It is not possible to engage in the direct apostolate without being a soul of prayer. We must be aware of oneness with Christ, as He was aware of oneness with His Father. Our activity is truly apostolic only in so far as we permit Him to work in us and through us, with His power, with His desire, with His love. We must become holy, not because we want to feel holy, but because Christ must be able to live His life fully in us.

We are to be all love, all faith, all purity, for the sake of the poor we serve. And once we have learned to seek God and His will, our contacts with the poor will become the means of great sanctity to ourselves and to others.

Love to pray—feel often during the day the need for prayer, and take trouble to pray. Prayer enlarges the heart until it is capable of containing God's gift of Himself. Ask and seek, and your heart will grow big enough to receive Him and keep Him as your own.

ON LOVE OF GOD

"Thou shalt love the Lord thy God with thy whole heart, with thy whole soul and with thy whole mind." This is the commandment of the great God, and He cannot command the impossible. Love is a fruit in season at all times, and within reach of every hand. Anyone may gather it and no limit is set. Everyone can reach this love through meditation, spirit of prayer and sacrifice, by an intense inner life.

DAILY PRAYER OF THE CO-WORKERS
OF MOTHER TERESA

Make us worthy, Lord, to serve our fellow men throughout the world who live and die in poverty and hunger. Give them, through our hands, this day their daily bread, and by our understanding love, give peace and joy.

Lord, make me a channel of Thy peace that, where there is hatred, I may bring love; that where there is wrong, I may bring the spirit of forgiveness; that where there is discord, I may bring harmony; that where there is error, I may bring truth; that where there is doubt, I may bring faith; that where there is despair, I may bring hope; that where there are shadows, I may bring light; that where there is sadness, I may bring joy.

Lord, grant that I may seek rather to comfort than to be comforted, to understand than to be understood; to love than to be loved; for it is by forgetting self that one finds; it is by forgiving that one is forgiven; it is by dying that one awakens to eternal life.

NOOR-UN-NISÂ INAYAT KHAN

The story of Noor-un-nisa Inayat Khan, daughter of the Sufi sage Hazrat Inayat Khan, was once little known outside of Sufi circles, but through the publication of the best-seller, **A Man Called Intrepid,** *Noor-un-nisa has become an inspiration for thousands throughout the world.*

Noor-un-nisa

Perhaps of all women saints, we can identify most easily with Noor-un-nisa, because she lived "in the world" in the West, in our time. And our hearts open up to her because of the unbelievable brutality to which she was subjected.

The key to her being is in her name, which means light of womanhood. *Noor* is the condition of our being when we have been totally purified of ourself, making us transparent to the *Noor-al-Anwar*, the light of lights or divine Intelligence, the light that makes all things clear. This condition arises when there is nothing we wish for and when we have no opinions, doubts, fears, inadequacies, or reservations. The real meaning of purity is not washing something away, but returning to one's original condition which is light. The effect of Noor-un-nisa's spirit is like having a bath of light.

Because of her sensitivity to suffering she has become a living signal. The purpose of suffering is to make people aware that there is something wrong, so it is in the nature of all living things that there should be an indication that there is something wrong. Some beings are chosen for this purpose; they are the Agnus Dei, the lamb of God. Hazrat Inayat Khan's words, "pain is my pleasure," express Noor-un-nisa's life, which is the eternal mission of compassion, to administer the balm of mercy upon life's wounded victims. Only those who have suffered in the extreme can understand the one who suffers and gives the message that there is still hope.

We are told by Noor's biographer that her interrogator said Noor was the best human being he had met in his life; that because of her, he believed in immortality. After knowing about Noor-un-nisa, it is very difficult to complain about life. Just the thought of her pulls us out of the quagmire of self-pity into the joy of overcoming.

> During the final days of World War II, a captured Resistance member sat alone in a black prison cell, tired, hungry, tortured and convinced of approaching death. After weeks of torture and torment, the prisoner was sure that there was no hope, that no one knew or cared. But in the middle of the night the door of the cell opened, and the jailer, shouting abuse into the darkness, threw a loaf of bread onto the dirt floor. The prisoner, by this time ravenous, tore open the loaf.
>
> Inside, there was a matchbox. Inside this matchbox, there were matches and a scrap of paper. The prisoner lit a match. On the paper there was a single word: *Corragio! Corragio.* Take courage. Don't give up, don't give in. We are trying to help you. *Corragio!* (Amnesty International)

Noor-un-nisa represents the living flame of courage, waiting to illuminate our suffering.

Memories of My Sister

PIR VILAYAT INAYAT KHAN

Near the gate of Fazal Manzil, Hazrat Inayat Khan's home in Suresnes, France, stands a memorial plaque bearing the name Noor Inayat Khan.

Ici habitait NOOR INAYAT KHAN
1914-1944
Madeleine dans la Resistance
Fusillee a Dachau
operatrice-radio des reseaux Buckmaster
Croix de Guerre 1939-1945   George Cross

Here lived Noor Inayat Khan
1914-1944
Called Madeleine in the Resistance
Shot at Dachau
Radio operator for the Buckmaster network

She stood out among her schoolmates for her shyness. Her mysterious and luminous glance and slightly tanned face could not fail to attract notice. Undoubtedly she was intimidated by the teasing directed against any unfamiliar child, yet she answered with an understanding and winning smile. One could hardly believe that her mother was a blonde

---

Pir Vilayat Inayat Khan is author of Toward the One *and* The Message in Our Time *and head of the Sufi Order in the West.*

American with blue eyes, if it were not for certain hardly discernible features. Her father had come from India and settled in Suresnes. This Eastern sage drew people from all corners of the world to Suresnes.

She so greatly gained the affection of her school pals that they elected her for the prize of "good comradeship." When she was twelve years old, after the Master's death, she became a little mother to her brothers and sisters, as her mother was committed to bed for years, suffering from the physical symptoms of a broken heart. All those who knew her had a deep respect for her and were moved by some endearing feature of her being. Was it because she so deeply cared for all those she came across—even her jailers?

During the Second World War, this gentle girl distinguished herself by her courage as one of the heroes of the French Resistance. And yet, in the middle of her greatest acts of courage she was afraid, which makes her extreme courage the more remarkable. This should embolden those who are afraid of being cowards when tested.

On the eve of the war, Noor and I conferred deeply and at length on the pros and cons of our participation in the war. The problem was the same question asked today by conscientious objectors. We had been formed at the school of our father, an Eastern sage and teacher. Behind him lay the entire tradition of Eastern spirituality. The then budding Gandhian non-violent campaign had proven its effectiveness as a means of confronting violence but was barely explored in the West. And was this not the message of Christ? Was there not a contradiction in killing in order to stop manslaughter? But suppose a Nazi should hold hostages at gunpoint and starve them to death; it would be complicity in their murder if, having the means to kill the Nazi and unable to otherwise prevent him from carrying out his deed, we abstained from doing it in the name of non-violence. As we had that conversation, could we have ever imagined that one day Noor would find herself in the plight of the people she wanted to save?

In the face of the extermination of Jews, how could one preach spiritual morality without actively participating in preventive action? The secret behind Noor's courage was the spiritual power inspired by our father, Hazrat Inayat Khan: spiritual idealism in action, not just in words.

After our exodus from Paris, the convoys of cars were mowed down by the machine guns of the Nazi pilots zooming at ground level during the embarkation at Bordeaux. We volunteered, Noor in the secret service network linking up with the French underground, the Maquis, I as a fighter pilot in the Royal Air Force. The secret service discovered in Noor the ideal agent: she was bilingual and knew the French territory and French customs and so gentle that nobody could have suspected her daring.

During the intensive training at the limits of human endurance, Noor distinguished herself by her perseverance. So much depended upon the leverage applied by the French Underground from inside. At the critical moment before the D-Day landing in Normandy she remained the last radio operator on the Continent, ensuring the last link between the Allied Headquarters and the French Underground. The life and death of millions and the fate of generations after the war was to depend upon one spirited by the vocation of a hero who accepted the risk of the supreme sacrifice: torture.

She was denounced by a "friend," a sister of a colleague in the network who sold information about her whereabouts to the Gestapo for a fee of approximately one thousand francs. The annals of her interrogation are silent about the torture, but one gleans echoes that are filled with terror. Her attempts to escape resulted in her being chained in a cold prison in Pforzheim with one bowl of soup daily, made out of potato peel. Her ordeal lasted until the very moment when, as the

Allies advanced into West German territory, they discovered the horrors of the concentration camp. She was immolated at the extermination camp of Dachau a few days before the Allies rescued those few who could still be saved from the carnage. A witness affirms having seen the gauleiter try to coerce her into saying, "Heil Hitler." She refused, saying, "The day will come when you will see the truth," wherefore she was whipped to death.

Today as teeming millions enjoy the luxury or at least the comfort attendant upon the gift of peace, do we realize that we owe this well-being to a few who have accepted the unimaginable suffering out of love for us while most of us have forgotten them?

Are we aware that, today in many countries, untold numbers of "prisoners of conscience," political prisoners, are subjected to interrogation and torture and thrown into jail without a trial and without the means of legitimate defense or appeal and without any means of communicating with the "outer world." Any person of good faith cannot but be indignated; but why do the large majority fail to do anything to allay this cruelty? Many argue that it happens in faraway countries; besides that they do not have the right to intervene in national problems and, what is more, they would not know how to go about it. Understandably, we do not wish to "mind other people's business" as far as their national politics are concerned, but when it comes to suffering imposed upon our fellow men, we are accomplices if we fail to do everything within our means to prevent this happening. One remembers the words of Pasteur: "I do not ask for from where you come, but what is your suffering."

In fact, it is possible to intervene effectively. The means of action is Amnesty International, an organization awarded

consultative status with the United Nations, which was recently awarded the Nobel Prize and which has contributed towards rescuing up to the present over 13,000 prisoners of conscience simply by altering public opinion, getting supporters to flood the authorities of the respective governments with thousands of letters and telegrams deputing lawyers and imploring the intervention of ambassadors and the press.

Each person will bring his active contribution to this appeal for mercy according to the measure of his conscience and his dedication to the human family and his love for his fellow man.

Song to Noor-un-nisa

ELIZABETH RECHTSCHAFFEN

She came to us an angel,
Longing for the light—
Daughter of the Prophet,
Lost in the stories that she found in the garden
And who was calling her.

Her child world of wonder
Drifted with the stream,
Until the words of someone older
Broke her dreams.

> *Noor-un-nisa, I have seen you*
> *Veiled in starlight with your father.*
> *You have shown my soul a thousand times*
> *The ecstasy of pain.*
> *And I bow before your beauty,*
> *Yes, I bow before your beauty*
> *Like a white rose in the rain.*

She opened up her heart
To ancient sorrow—
Princess of the Messenger.
Turned from the garden to face a world on fire,
And who was calling her.

She crossed the stormy waters.
She crossed the flaming skies.
On the flying wind
She heard the human cries.

Noor-un-nisa, I have seen you
Veiled in starlight with your father.
You have shown my soul a thousand times
The ecstasy of pain.
And I bow before your beauty,
Yes, I bow before your beauty
Like a white rose in the rain.

In the darkened streets of Paris,
A soldier of the light,
She kept her secrets hidden,
Finding the peace she had lost in the garden,
And who was calling her.

She could have fled
Before her jailers found her,
But Noor-un-nisa heard the angels sigh.
And even those who took her life were startled
By the gentleness and courage
In her eyes.

Noor-un-nisa, I have seen you
Veiled in starlight with your father.
You have shown my soul a thousand times
The ecstasy of pain.
And I bow before your beauty,
Yes, I bow before your beauty
Like a white rose in the rain.

The music for this song can be obtained by writing Elizabeth Rechtschaffen, Box 396, New Lebanon, N.Y. 12125.

The Veiled One

There are cosmic beings who are so hidden that it is not possible to reach them unless one comes into a deeply receptive condition, attuning far beyond the created worlds. They dwell in the spheres of prayer and glorification, rapt in a continual vibration of silence and peace. Such a being is the one known only as the Veiled One.

She is an embodiment of all that is precious, all that is valued, and all that is sacred: she is the ideal. To value an ideal, one has to die for it and one has to dedicate one's life to it. No one can know it intellectually, but only through experience. When the ideal becomes a reality, it is the Veiled One inside your heart. Before that it may be a concept but not yet a reality. You may strive for it, betray it, doubt it, deviate from it, but once you have been tested for your ideal by the test of death—in which your self dies so that your ideal may live—then it becomes a reality and you live by that reality. You become just a cover over that reality.

Thy Light hath illuminated the dark chambers of my mind; Thy love is rooted in the depths of my heart; Thine own eyes are the light of my soul; Thy power worketh behind my action; Thy peace alone is my life's repose; Thy Will is behind my every impulse; Thy voice is audible in the words I speak; Thine own image is my countenance. My body is but a cover over Thy soul; my life is Thy very breath, my Beloved, and myself is Thine own Being.

(Hazrat Inayat Khan, *The Complete Sayings*)

The Veiled One is brighter than ten thousand suns and yet when she is contemplated she covers herself with ten thousand veils and becomes as pale as the moon to protect you against her brightness. She is so fragile that a breath of air could disperse her to the winds. Her strength is in her spirit which is undaunted. She is passive only to the will of God.

When a woman discovers the Veiled One within herself, the Veiled One appears as the Mother of the World. When a man becomes conscious of the Veiled One, she appears as the Beloved. A woman becomes her embodiment and a man becomes her protector.

The Veiled One Speaks

PIR VILAYAT INAYAT KHAN

My voice has to cross a thousand veils before it reaches the heart of man. These veils are not only built up by the contempt of primitive man for womanhood, but also by the incomprehension of more evolved men toward the special quality of womanliness and the declining faith of women in the veiled values of womanhood, distracted as they are by the more apparent ones.

The inner veils are created by me for protection because I must be fragile to be receptive to the divine Voice. I am in the depth of my Lord and Master. He becomes my Voicepiece when He speaks from the depth of His Being. He draws from my soul when I am in communion with God.

I abstain from competing and from using argument as a weapon since it only reaches the surface of beings and fails to leave a lasting mark. There are special moments when I have to communicate without the medium of my Lord and Master. A heart-to-heart talk must be direct. The voice of the heart is studded with tears because the heart is the broken shell that gives new birth. Pearls are the tears that rise out of the pain of the oyster.

When I speak, I stir the hearts of all beings and bring them to themselves in the depth which they had long evaded. I am the sacrificed one who gives life, I am the Holy Sacrament of the *Rassoul* (prophet), the quintessence of His very substance, offered and shared, yet forever mysterious, tasted yet unknown.

Mother of the World

The vastness of the Mother of the World makes it possible to experience her only as an archetype although she is a reality: the eternal feminine aspect of God, hidden and fragile yet most powerful. She is one being and she is many beings; she is the depth of all beings, she is the veil of God. She can only be known by diving into the ocean of silence.

To understand the female aspect of God, we must come into a purely passive condition. We may then be able to feel the presence of the Mother of the World. The Mother of the World is the soul of the prophet. She is always hidden giving birth to the souls of the children of the new age, particularly those to be born on planet earth.

We must be careful not to step on the toes of new age women by saying that God is male, because this cannot be understood by the mind or even the soul. The female is contained within the male in origin, then the male emerges from the female at the end. The female embodies and the male becomes embodied.

The Mother of the World is always veiled. That is why she is unknown and has never been stressed until recently. By stressing her, one tries to bring her out of her seclusion, and she does not wish to be brought out of her seclusion, because she is rapt in the love of God. Few realize that one cannot reach God except through her because she has become so transparent as to be invisible.

She reflects the love of God that only a woman understands (or the Messenger, who has also become passive towards God). Her invisibility emphasizes that she is nothing except in her Lord; vision gives the semblance of being and strengthens the ego of the viewer.

The Mother of the World's heart, symbolized by the Holy Grail, is the reservoir of love for the universe. She transforms love into compassion and compassion into love. She transforms the sadness of human suffering, which is giving birth to God, into the joy of resurrecting Him on earth. By becoming the essence of the essence of the essence, one ends up being nothing: absorbed in the one consciousness of God.

Why do people want to give a place to the Mother of the World when she doesn't want a place, give her a personality when she doesn't wish to have a personality, figure her when she doesn't wish to be figured, and make her an object of vision when she doesn't wish to be seen? The ego wants to see itself projected in an eternal principle and an image of itself. But the Mother of the World is not an image because she is too real to be an image. She breaks every image that is imposed upon her because she wants to identify with her Lord and Master. She couldn't bear to have any image other than His or to represent any principle that people like to give her. For her there is just the oneness, and one cannot find the oneness by promoting her against her will.

BIBLIOGRAPHY

Anandashram. *Guru's Grace: Autobiography of Mother Krishnabai.* Kanhangad, South India: Anandashram P.O. 670531, 1964.

Anandashram. *Silver Jubilee Souvenir of Mother Krishnabai's Renunciation.* Kanhangad, South India: Anandashram P.O. 670531, 1955.

Asch, Sholem. *Mary.* New York: G.P. Putnam's Sons, 1949.

*Atmaprana, Pravrajika. *Sister Nivedita.* Calcutta: Sister Nivedita Girls School, 1961.

Brunton, Paul. *A Search in Secret India.* New York: Samuel Weiser, Inc.

*Fuller, Jean Overton. *Noor-un-nisa Inayat Khan [Madeleine].* Rotterdam: East-West Publications Fonds N.V., 1971.

Michael, Arnold. *Blessed Among Women: A Metaphysical Portrayal of the Feminine Principle.* Santa Monica: De Vorss & Co., 1973. Available from Sufi Order Ojai Center, c/o Rahima Sommers, Box 5145, Ojai, California 93023. Tells the life of Mary.

*Muggeridge, Malcolm. *Something Beautiful for God.* Scranton: Ballantine, 1971.
The story of Mother Teresa.

*Ramakrishna Vedanta Center. *Women Saints of East and West.* London: 1955.
Available from Vedanta Press, 1946 Vedanta Place, Hollywood, California 90068.

*Smith, Margaret. *Rabia, the Mystic, A.D. 717-801, and her Fellow Saints of Islam.* London: Cambridge University Press, 1928.

Stevenson, William. *A Man Called Intrepid.* New York: Harcourt Brace Jovanovich, 1976. First edition.

*Available from the Abode Store, Box 396, New Lebanon, NY 12125.

MEDITATION

Woman is the steppingstone to God's sacred altar.
[*Hazrat Inayat Khan*]

Meditation

Although the Divine Presence is a reality in the depth of every human, unless we open ourselves to its action, it remains dormant. Similarly, grace and effort are two poles of spiritual transformation. This section deals with what we can *do* to help create the emotional, mental, and spiritual environment conducive to transformation. Most of the exercises can be done both individually and in a group. Group work brings more challenges in the area of harmony and attunement, but what is achieved no doubt exceeds the individual experience since the current cosmic note is unity. Therefore I would recommend working in groups of women with these meditations.

If you intend to start a women's meditation group, it is important first to arrive at a level of sympathetic harmony. After a great deal of experience, I've come to realize that the basic sympathy and sincerity of all members of the group toward one another is the only foundation for spiritual work. Although some kinds of group work thrive on tension, and certain artistic endeavors seem to require conflict as a means to further unfoldment, in women's meditation, requiring very high attunements, there is no room for disharmony. Therefore work out all personality problems as they arise, keep your hearts free from psychic build-up and negative thoughts or any kind of pettiness.

Group channeling requires the dissolving of the individual in the group consciousness for the duration of the meditation. If women are not prepared to be sisters in the highest sense, the work is simply blocked. *I cannot over-emphasize the need for true friendship in spiritual group work.* Remember Christ's words when He was asked how His disciples would be recognized: "by their love."

Purification

The first and most important step in spiritual unfoldment is purification. One could even say that purification is all that is necessary since the divine Perfection is a reality at the core of our being and everything else is just a cover. We can start the purifying process in the physical body by improving the diet, by abstaining from alcohol and drugs, by maintaining a rhythmic pattern of repose and activity, and by keeping the body clean through daily ablutions.

We should be aware of the important process of mental purification. This consists of cleansing the mind of impurities and all undesirable impressions. Then comes the purification of the heart, the great Sufi science through which we uncover the divine intention working through us. The process of purification reaches its fulfillment when we become aware that ultimate and final purification means freeing the universal I AM consciousness, the Only Being, from any consciousness of limitation imposed by an individualized consciousness.

Hazrat Inayat Khan points out that exaltation itself is a type of purification. "A moment's exaltation can purify the evil of many years, because it is like bathing in the Ganges, as Hindus say." There are three levels of exaltation. These can be used as themes for contemplation:

There is a physical aspect of exaltation which comes as a reaction or result of having seen the immensity of space, having looked at the wide horizon, or having seen the clear sky, the moonlit night and nature at dawn. Looking at the rising sun, watching the setting sun, looking at the world from the top of a mountain, all these experiences, even such an experience as watching the little smiles of an innocent infant.

A higher aspect of exaltation is a moral exaltation—when we are sorry for having said or done something unpleasant; when we have asked forgiveness and humbled ourselves before someone towards whom we were inconsiderate. We have humbled our pride then. Or when we felt a deep gratitude to someone who had done something for us; when we have felt love, sympathy, or devotion which seems endless and which seems so great that our heart cannot accommodate it; when we have felt so much pity for someone that we have forgotten ourselves; when we have found a profound happiness in rendering a humble service to someone in need; when we have said a prayer which has come from the bottom of our heart; when we have realized our own limitation and smallness in comparison with the greatness of God.

The third aspect of exaltation comes by touching the reason of reasons and by realizing the essence of wisdom; by feeling the depth, the profound depth of one's heart; by widening one's outlook on life; by broadening one's conception, by deepening one's sympathies, and by soaring upwards to those spheres where spiritual exaltation manifests.(Hazrat Inayat Khan)

It does not take much to make us exalted:
a kind attitude, a sympathetic trend of mind,
and it is already there. If we were to notice it,
we would find that our eyes shed tears
in sympathy with another, we were already exalted,
our soul has bathed in the spiritual Ganges.
                          [Hazrat Inayat Khan]

Crystal, what are you?
  I am the shadow of Christ's heart.
What quality do you possess?
  I am empty of self, so that by gazing, one sees
    in me His heart reflected.

(Hazrat Inayat Khan, *The Complete Sayings*)

Meditation on a Crystal

The crystal represents a certain perfection in the mineral kingdom. When used as an object of concentration it can stimulate the purification process. Because it typifies the immaculate virginal state, it is a natural concentration for women's meditation.

Place a crystal in the center of a circle of women on a stand at eye level in such a way that the sunlight is reflected through it, illuminating it. The light of the crystal is the shadow of the Christ light, that light which is never corrupted because of the innocence of its receptacle. The goal of this meditation is complete transfiguration. There is no use in concentrating on light unless you can allow your whole being—body, mind, heart, and soul—to be transfigured by light, so that you are no longer able to remain the same person.

· · · · ·

As you begin to gaze at the crystal, you may make the mistake of devouring it with your aggressive "looking." Gradually you become aware that in this practice the secret is to become passive to the force of the light working upon you. Open yourself wide—what are you afraid of?

· · · · ·

Experience your body becoming transparent. Gaze at the crystal, then close your eyes and experience your organs, cells, bones, and flesh becoming transparent. You may experience the decaying effect of lifeless food and drugs that have robbed your physical body of its magnetism and light. Realize that down to your very flesh, you are the temple of God and a receptacle of the Holy Spirit. Cleanse your chakras with light. Feel your aura. Let light flow like rivers through your eyes transforming them into the glance of Truth.

. . . . .

Experience your mind becoming crystal clear. Gaze at the crystal, shut your eyes, and realize that clarity of mind emerges out of rigorously controlled thoughts: no slackness, no wallowing in the fantasies of the ego. Nor is the illuminated mind in a trance; it sees the intention of God behind every being, thing, and event.

. . . . .

Experience your heart becoming transparent. Look at the crystal, then close your eyes once more and feel your heart. Is it transparent? Why not? Darkness is born out of doubt and despondency, self-pity, criticizing, feelings of inadequacy, anger, trying to conceal weaknesses, or even taking pride in them. All these things are obstacles to light and must be removed. Are there still shadows? Give up your personal pain. The universe is yours and you are niggardly about some trivial personal pain that is based on the narrowness of human consciousness! The vehicle must be sensitive but not small. If you offer a small chalice you limit the divine bounty.

. . . . .

Now experience cosmic emotion. Realize that in love you cannot own another being; give each being freedom and appreciate the beauty of that being without possessing it. Go deeper and deeper, commune with the heart of the universe, the heart of God, and experience compassion for all beings. Experience the living miracle of light!

. . . . .

Now experience the colors fading into translucent, glistening ice: the landscape of the soul. Enter *by becoming* the living temple that has been created by your sisterhood in light. Let your heart be revivified by the power of the Holy Spirit as it descends upon the living altar formed out of your hearts merged in sympathy and common dedication to the service of the forces of light bringing about the transformation of earth and the restoration of the Kingdom of God.

Amen

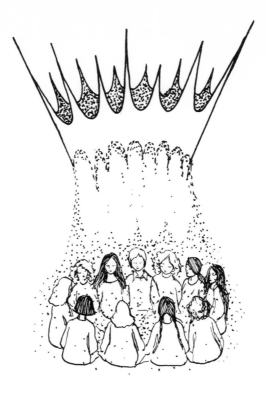

The Temple of Light Meditation

The purpose of the Temple of Light Meditation is to bring universal light to the earth plane through group attunement, which also brings about personal transformation. It can be done as a regular part of a woman's class or separately as a ritual.

The group must be purified through breathing practices, sharings from the heart, mantras, prayers, or music. When unity and purity are reached, the circle of women, dressed in white, should sit facing center. A group leader or spokeswoman begins to guide the practice.

Awareness will be first of the physical unity of the circle. Experience the body as a state of the spirit that has emerged through evolution and contains the whole planetary and heavenly history. Begin to feel the unity of all bodies hatched out of the clay of planet earth. Lose the sense of individuality, even on the physical plane.

Then be aware of the emotions of sympathy and dedication that have drawn you together. Experience the dissolving of individual hearts into the Great Heart and feel the presence of overwhelming love, the essence of the Divine Mother.

As greater unity is achieved and consciousness rises very high, become aware of the group crown center that is forming in the center of the circle above your heads. Then begin to draw light through the unified crown down onto the altar of the heart and radiate out in all directions. Feel like a many-faceted crystal with light pouring through you.

Then close with a silent prayer of gratitude. Be careful never to dwell in personal satisfaction when channeling light.

You will come to realize that everything you do or think during your daily life affects the few moments you spend during the Temple of Light Meditation. Judgments made about people, anger, lack of self-control, and all the other weeds we wish to eradicate from the garden of our personality all prevent the passage of light through us. So this simple practice will have the amazing effect of impelling you to transform your character and daily life.

THE HIGH PRIESTESS

THE EMPRESS.

The High Priestess
and the Empress

As a means of discovering our receptive and expressive natures, let us look for a moment at the archetypes of the High Priestess and the Empress.

THE HIGH PRIESTESS represents our deepest inner self, the part of us turned within, responsive to the unmanifest life. The High Priestess listens to the voice of silence; she is the embodiment of intuition. When we still our body, mind, and emotions, a door opens into the unseen world. The High Priestess is the guardian of the inner knowledge. The Bible speaks of the ''still small voice.'' This voice is only heard in the depth, far away from the noise of the world. The state of receptivity is the key to this knowledge.

Just as the reflection of the moon is greatly distorted by the ruffled waves of the lake, the experience of the inner reality is distorted when it passes through the aperture of our individual being which is limited by our personal viewpoint. The great art of the High Priestess is stillness: to become like a mirror so the deeper worlds can be reflected in the lake of the heart.

The following Sufi story illustrates the art of the High Priestess:

> We were once, one substance, like the sun: flawless we were and pure as water is pure. Purify yourself, therefore, from the qualities of self, so that you may see your essence, perfect and pure. If you seek for a parable of the knowledge which is hidden, hear the story of the Greeks and the Chinese.
>
> The Chinese said, "We are the better artists," and the Greeks rejoined, "We have more skill than you and more sense of beauty."
>
> So the king in whose presence they were speaking said to them, "I will test you in this, to see which of you is justified in your claim."
>
> The Chinese said, "Give us a room for ourselves and let there be a room for the Greeks." There were two rooms, with doors opposite each other; the Chinese took one room and the Greeks took the other. The Chinese asked the king for a hundred different colors. The king opened his treasure house for them to take what they would. Each morning the Chinese took from the treasure house some of the gift of colors.
>
> But the Greeks said, "No colors or paints are needed for our work which is only to remove the rust." They shut themselves in and polished continuously, until all was pure and clear like the sky. Many colors are like a cloud, and freedom from color like the moon. Whatever radiance and light you see in the cloud, know that it comes from the stars and the moon and the sun.
>
> When the Chinese had finished their work, they rejoiced and began to beat the drums. The king came in and looked and he was dumbfounded. Then after that, he came to the Greeks. One of them lifted the curtain that was between the rooms. The reflection of those paintings the Chinese had done fell upon those polished walls. All that the king had seen there seemed more lovely here: the wonder of it made his eyes start out of their sockets. (Jelaluddin Rumi)

Traditionally, the High Priestesses were kept in isolation, without contact with the outside world. They were the vestal virgins, dedicated to becoming channels for the inner voice. Secluded, celibate, and vegetarian, they were so sensitized as to become the harp through which the universe speaks. The priests then interpreted this knowledge. However, to women in the new age, it is no longer satisfactory to be passive channels; the goal of woman today is to embody in her whole personality and life the wisdom she channels.

Women whose personalities show the High Priestess condition, but who have not developed spiritually or attained a degree of mastery of this condition, may tend to be aloof, cold, or critical, which comes from a basic lack of attunement to the world. On the other hand, she may be oversensitive to impressions and people, even to the point of becoming unable to cope with life at all. She is impressionable but has not learned to direct her receptivity inward and ends up being at the mercy of the situations and people. These are the negative aspects of her personality, but this same aloneness and sensitivity directed positively can unfold the High Priestess' potential inner knowledge, clarity, insight, and intuition.

Since we are taking archetypal traits out of the context of the whole integrated being for the sake of study, we must be aware of the possibility of distortion when qualities are taken out of context by the total personality.

THE EMPRESS, on the other hand, is the part of our being that expresses, acts, and gives. She is pictured in the Tarot cards pregnant and surrounded by luscious, ripe fruit trees. If the High Priestess represents the crescent moon state, the Empress represents the full moon state: that moment of extreme fullness when expression is not premeditated but inevitable.

The High Priestess responds and the Empress expresses. She is the fertile earth forever giving out of love with no thought of return; she is the sun shining upon the deserving and undeserving alike; she is the queen who sustains her kingdom, made up of all those beings who come within her enfoldment. She gives and asks nothing in return; all souls respond to her. She is the body of Christ offered in the sacrament of the Last Supper.

This ancient Oriental tale illustrates the condition of the Empress:

> Far, far in the sandy desert was a small oasis of palm trees and flowers. And in that oasis, as a lonely hermit, lived an elephant, a beautiful elephant. He ate the fruit of the trees, and drank from a little stream of water that ran through the rocks. Happy he was dancing through the banana-trees, watching day and night come over the desert.
>
> But one day, as he was dancing alone, in the distance some strange voices came to his ears. "Whose are those voices?" he said to himself. "Are they not voices of men, of unhappy men? Who are those men, and why do they cross the desert? Surely they are lost, or maybe they suffer some terrible pain."
>
> Such were the thoughts of the handsome elephant as he walked in the direction of the voices. He walked some distance over the burning sand when he came upon a great crowd of men all huddled together at death's door, and at the piteous sight his eyes, for the first time in his happy life, filled with tears.
>
> "Oh, travellers," he said in a tender voice, "wherefrom do you come, and where are you going? Have you lost your way in the desert? Tell me, O men, that I may help you in some way."
>
> So happy were the men to hear these friendly words that they fell on their knees before him.
>
> "Beautiful one," they said, "we have been driven from our country by our king and have roamed through the desert for many days. Not a drop of water have we found to drink, nor food to give us strength. Help us, O dear one," they cried. "Help us."
>
> "How many are you?" asked the elephant.
>
> "We were one thousand," they replied, "but many have perished on the way."

The elephant gazed at them. One was crying for water, another asking for food. "You are weak, O men," he said, "and the next city is too far for you to reach without food and water. Therefore walk towards the hill which stands before you. At its foot you will find the body of a large elephant which will provide you with food, and nearby runs a stream of sweet water."

When he had thus spoken he ran over the burning sand and disappeared as he had come. Where did the great elephant go? And why did he run at such a pace? Straight to the hill he went, to the same hill he had pointed out to the men, but he took another way, that the men might not see him going. He climbed to the top of the hill and then from its highest point, in a mighty jump, his beautiful body crashed to the ground below.

When the men reached the spot they gazed at the giant-like form and a great fear seized them.

"Is this not our dear elephant?" exclaimed one among them.

"This face is the same face, the eyes, though closed, are the same eyes," said another.

And they all sat in the sand and wept bitterly. After some time one of them spoke. "Companions," he said, "we cannot eat this elephant who has given his life for his friends."

"Nay, friends," said another, "if we do not eat this elephant his sacrifice will have been useless, and we shall die before reaching the next city. Thus we shall not be helped, nor shall the wish of our elephant be fulfilled."

The men spoke no more but bent their heads in the burning sand and ate the meat with tears in their eyes. And it made them strong, very strong, so that they were able to cross the desert and reach a town where their troubles came to an end. They never forgot the great elephant, and they lived happy ever after. (Noor-un-nisa Inayat Khan, "The Great Elephant," from *Twenty Jataka Tales*.)

Of course the Empress also has her distorted image in the personality of those women who have not attained the higher octave of her being and manifest only her outgoing energy. These women may give of themselves compulsively, belonging to ten committees and frantically seeking recogni-

81

tion from their activity. They burden their children, husbands, and friends with a very heavy self-oriented love.

Perhaps you can now see that the saving grace of the Empress would be the High Priestess' ability to attune to the inner depth for inspiration and guidance to direct her activity, and that the great abundant love streaming from the heart of the Empress will save the High Priestess from the lonely isolation of her ivory tower. As perfection comes through balance, the way of the new age woman is attaining the proper balance of these energies. This balance means that women overcome the jarring influences of life by attuning to the deeper side of life and therein receiving inspiration and direction in order to live, create, and enrich our own lives and the lives of those around us. Toward the One, united with all.

CONCENTRATIONS TO DEVELOP THE QUALITIES
OF THE HIGH PRIESTESS

Concentrate on the image of a crescent moon.
The symbol represents an inner reality to be discovered.
Use the symbol as a steppingstone to discover this part of you.
Feel the emotion of alert emptiness.

Experience yourself as a mirror, completely passive.
You may be surprised to discover that this is not a lifeless state,
  but one of being totally alert and concentrated, but devoid
  of any reference to your self as an entity.
Feel the emotion of clarity.
Experience yourself becoming whatever passes before you.

Think of a being.
Imagine every detail of personality and form.
Then imagine that you are sitting before that person
  like a mirror.
Experience that being reflected in you
  until there is no difference.
[Do this also with a flower or a crystal.]

Feel your heart to be a lake.
Become calm and peaceful with no thoughts.
As you exhale, smooth the surface of this lake in the heart
    until it is as calm as glass.
One has to release emotions and disturbing thoughts
    which are the cause of the waves.
As the lake becomes crystal clear,
    imagine a five-pointed star reflected in absolute clarity
    upon the surface of the still lake.

Close the ears with the fingertips.
Listen with the inner ears [the temples]
    to the sound of the spheres,
    the sounds made by the spinning of the planets,
    the sounds of the turning of the sunflowers,
    and all the sounds of the universe.
Extend hearing.

Sit with a partner.
Each partner in turn thinks of a form [circle, square, or triangle]
    or a color.
The other partner practices becoming blank and allowing
    the form or color to be projected to her.
First you will be tempted to use your mind,
    but through practice you will learn to use your intuition.
Fear of failure is active and destroys intuition.

In a group of a few women, place a veil over one [each in turn].
The rest should pass before her one at a time;
*   she should try to feel the qualities of the person before her.*
Again, she will have to develop her subtle perception
*   in order to succeed.*

Meditate with the music of Allegri [see music section].

CONCENTRATIONS TO DEVELOP THE QUALITIES OF THE EMPRESS

Concentrate on a star which represents the expression of light.

Feel the opening of the heart
*   by experiencing your heart center as a rose*
*   that is slowly unfolding and spreading its perfume.*
[This is especially good to do with the music of
*   Canon in D by Pachelbel.]*

Every day, do an act of selfless service for someone
  without feeling pride in yourself for having done it.

Walking exercise:
Walk with the feeling that you are the entire planet,
  with rivers, forests, and fields of food.
Feel as if all beings are living and growing out of you.
Know what it is to give and sustain life.

Walking exercise:
Walk with the concentration of being
  just at the point of giving birth
  or with the concentration of a fruit tree
  laden with fruit that is just about to fall.

Concentrate on your heart overflowing with love for all beings.
"With the thought of love let me contemplate the world."

CONCENTRATIONS FOR BALANCE OF QUALITIES

Walking exercise:
Walk with the left hand open in a receiving position
*   and the right hand palm forward in a giving position.*
Feel both energies at the same time, in perfect balance.

In meditation feel light entering the open crown center,
*   descending upon the heart, and radiating outwards,*
*   like a temple.*

If you receive an inspiration,
*   carry it out in life in a concrete way.*

If you love someone, do an act of service for them.

Music, the word we use in our everyday language, is nothing less than the picture of our Beloved. It is because music is a picture of our Beloved that we love music. But the question is what is our Beloved and where is our Beloved? Our Beloved is that which is our source and goal, and what we see of our Beloved before our physical eyes is the beauty which is before us; and that part of our Beloved not manifest to our eyes is that inner form of beauty of which our Beloved speaks to us. If only we would listen to the voice of all beauty that attracts us in any form, we would find that in every aspect it tells us that behind all manifestation is the perfect Spirit, the spirit of wisdom. [Hazrat Inayat Khan]

Music

One of the easiest and most effective means of higher attunement is music. Hazrat Inayat Khan says: "There is nothing in this world which can help one spiritually more than music. Meditation prepares, but music is the highest for touching perfection."

Although there are many ways to use music as a spiritual practice, such as chanting, singing, sound exercises, wazifas, and mantra, I would like to introduce to you the use of meditation to recorded music. This requires no training, talent, or leader, but one must enter into the state of consciousness that the music expresses. Some pieces express the vision of the mystic; others, the heavenly planes; another may express devotion or deep religious dedication. Each piece offers the unique opportunity of entering a new world of experience, but the listener must leave his own state and enter deeply—with mind, heart, and soul—into the music.

Allegri. *Miserere from Evensong for Ash Wednesday.* Argo Records, ZRG5365.
 Plane of the soul beyond creation, the immaculate state.

Bach, J.S. *Fifth Brandenburg Concerto in D Major*, BWV1050, part 1, Allegro. Columbia Records, M25-731, MS-6784.
 Expresses ecstasy and freedom; wonderful for dancing and spinning.

Bach, J.S. *Concerto in C Minor for Two Harpsichords and Orchestra*, BWV 1060, part 2, Adagio. Nonesuch Records, HE-73001.
Expresses perfect balance and harmony.

Bach. J.S. *Fantasia in C Minor*, BWV 537. Musical Heritage Society, MHS 600.
Expresses the mystic vision.

Bach, J.S. *Passacaglia and Fugue in C Minor*, BXV 582. From Vol. 3 of Organ Works, Musical Heritage Society, MHS 599.
Music of the spheres, atoms, and planets.

Gregorian Chant, Easter music sung by the Benedictine monks of the Abbey of St. Maurice and St. Maur. Philips Records, PHC 9004.
Perfect peace and prayer.

Gregorian Chant, sung by Russian Orthodox monks.

Monteverdi. *Mass for Four Voices* [*"Magnificat"*], Choir of St. John's College, Cambridge. Argo Records, ZRG 5494.

Pachelbel. *Canon in D Major.* Musical Heritage Society, MHS 1060.
Music of overcoming, rising, entering the world of light with a touch of nostalgia.

Purcell. *Miserere,* sung by Alfred Diller.
Expresses the depth of suffering.

Segal, Joseph and Nathan. "R 'Faynu" from *Hallel, Songs of Praise.* Joy of Movement Center, 23 Main St., Watertown, MA 02172.
True music of the heart, with the whole spirit of the Jewish race.

Tallis, Thomas. *Motets of Thomas Tallis.* Seraphim Records, S-60256.
The motet, Spem in Alum, *expresses the state of resurrection.*

Victoria. *Lamentations of Jeremiah,* sung by Scuola Di Chiesa. Pye Records Ltd., 1967, A.T.V. House, Great Cumberland Place, London, W1, England. (This European version is recommended over the Musical Heritage edition.)
Ideal for women's meditation. Very peaceful and beautiful.

This is Not My Body

(a round)

Words: Hazrat Inayat Khan   Music: Allaudin Mathieu

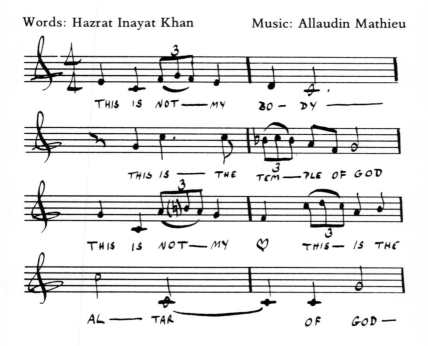

DAILY LIFE

The Sacred Concentration
of Pregnancy

The conception and carrying within of a being is a sacred concentration by which a soul is brought to earth and the mother is opened to the awareness of the inner planes. The relationship between mother and child begins before conception, when she may intuitively feel the presence of a soul who wishes to incarnate, though often this is unnoticed. Actually, it is the earth-bound soul who draws two beings together through mutual attraction and love in order to achieve its purpose of incarnation.

If conditions in life are such that two people decide to conceive a child, a conscious conception is a deep experience for the mother, father, and new soul. Preparation through purification, retreat, spiritual attunements, and prayer help to build a conducive environment for the earth-bound soul. Yet we must remember that the divine planning can also break through our own planning in unexpected ways, so you should not be upset if you find yourself unexpectedly pregnant when you weren't preparing or if, on the other hand, you have tried and tried and no pregnancy occurs. There are often physical reasons why conception does not occur. However, after trying methods advised by a physician and after making sure both parents are physically able to conceive, spiritual methods can sometimes be used to trigger off the ability to conceive.

In conscious conception, the awareness of the presence of the new soul gives love-making a vaster dimension. After sexual union, the actual meeting of the sperm and ovum can happen anytime within 72 hours. The mother, in a quiet and sensitive state, can experience the moment of this meeting within her body. More often this happens unnoticed because of the lifestyle of most modern women.

The greatest test for the new soul requires the sperm-ovum to attach itself firmly to the uterine wall with a great deal of strength, because the force of the monthly menstrual cycle is very powerful. Unless the desire and power of the incarnating soul is strong, the force of menstruation will wash away the growth. It takes the power and concentration of the soul to hold on at that moment. Many pregnancies (30 per cent) are lost at this time and, in fact, many women do not even know that they were pregnant. Once this test is past and the embryo is implanted in the womb, the miracle of the evolution of the physical body proceeds, directed by the innate intelligence evolved over the course of millions of years of physical life.

The soul is involved with the physical development of its body in greater or lesser degree depending upon the individual soul. The soul has already passed through many degrees of incarnation on higher levels: through the angelic planes of light and vibration and the jinn plane where talents, karma, personality, and life purpose are concretized. Some souls, even after their bodies have started growing on the earth plane, are very detached and spend little time in physical consciousness. Indeed, some souls take many years to incarnate fully on earth, even after the birth of their physical bodies.

Very sensitive or evolved souls from higher worlds find it difficult to relate to the physical plane. They are often unable to incarnate, or change their minds as they experience (in the womb) life on earth. This is a common reason for miscarriages.

Or sometimes plans change, and a soul needs to stay on another plane to fulfill a desire or obligation, and therefore a miscarriage occurs. Haven't we all at some time canceled a trip or changed our plans?

Sensitive souls are much more open to earth vibrations than we who have lived on earth and accustomed ourselves to them. I've heard quite often that a newly pregnant woman will have terrible, violent dreams which I believe represent the experience of the new soul as it penetrates the dense layers surrounding earth, for the actions and thoughts of all beings on earth form an aura around our planet. The shock of encountering the violent, materialistic aura often sends the more evolved souls back. For this reason, incarnating souls who are being sent with a special mission are sometimes (in emergency cases) anesthetized so that they experience very little of the earth plane, yet their bodies continue to be formed, nourished, and held by the silver chord that attaches the soul to the physical body. In such cases there is a nearly complete block between the physical body and the higher consciousness, which may take some time to integrate after birth.

I am convinced that certain "problem" or autistic children simply find incarnation too painful, so they refuse to unite the various levels of their being.

When these channels between spheres are closed down, the mother is also bound in her earth-plane consciousness, so that a woman who normally experiences deeper levels of reality, through meditation or spiritual evolution, is unable to be "high." If she wishes to contact a new soul or participate in the inner levels of incarnation, she must do samadhi types of meditation, leaving entirely the consciousness of the physical plane and experiencing reality in higher spheres. This is normally not advisable, as the goal of spiritual practice is a deep but *integrated* experience of reality.

The more joyous experience of pregnancy for the mother happens when there are no blockages and the channels between earth and the higher spheres are open. It is a highly illuminating time because she has access to these spheres which are normally closed to her. It is also a time of great mystical revelation for the mother because she is experiencing the act of creation right in her own being and her own body. She feels and experiences what God feels and experiences.

She may feel an undefinable sense of suffering that is not personal but cosmic and whose source is far beyond the created worlds. She may discover within herself the source of life as a glistening, bubbling spring emerging as single droplets out of the rocky grotto of Elijah, who is the patron saint of the waters of life. She feels the deep emotion that has caused the rocks to weep life, and she discovers how life is born out of suffering. Yet this very suffering contains the seeds of joy, for she knows that life offers the great opportunity of resurrection, whereby the silent, unmanifested Being becomes a concrete reality, while making her the Truth.

The mother may experience specific needs and desires at this time, in food, music, literature, or physical environment. These are the ways the descending soul begins to assert its personality and make sure its special needs are met even before birth.

The father can also play a part in the formation of the child. His protective aura gives nourishment and strength to the growing aura of the child. His understanding of the changes going on in the body and psyche of the mother gives her the security and peace she needs at this special time. But please remember that fathers need extra love and attention during pregnancy, too, because they often sense the mother's new detachment which is confusing if not hurtful to them. Never allow yourself to be so totally wrapped up in yourself that you do not attend to the needs of those around you.

Here are a few suggestions for concentrations during pregnancy:

During the entire pregnancy be particularly aware of obtaining nourishing, healthy food. Check with a physician for proper vitamins and calcium and minerals. Get plenty of exercise and fresh air.

Listen internally to the needs of the new soul; some need extra protection. Surround yourself with beauty and nice people and avoid anything ugly, gross, or dishonest.

Concentrate on a silver cord that passes from your crown center to the child's crown center. Surround your body, especially the womb, with a protective aura of light.

Concentrate on the Holy Spirit becoming life through you. Draw energy down through your crown, along the spine, and into the womb. Purify your aura daily through breathing practices and meditation.

Conscious pregnancy can be a deep fulfillment in the life of a woman. Remember to be grateful for the privilege of being the instrument of the manifestation of God on earth.

If the child does not make it to the earth, or dies shortly after birth, remember that there is always a reason, though because of the limitation of *our* understanding we cannot understand it. Have faith in the divine planning.

Birth

ELIZABETH RECHTSCHAFFEN

Labor, or the process of birthing a child, is the culmination of the experience of pregnancy and the beginning of the role of motherhood. In the hours of labor, the woman leaves the pregnant state and all of the inner, reclusive feelings that came along with pregnancy and enters the very vital world of mothering. I have attended many births as a labor coach and I never fail to marvel at that moment when receptivity and creativity meet: when the infant leaves the mother's womb and takes its first breath on earth. It is no wonder that such an intense process has attracted so much respect, superstition, and fear in different cultures throughout the ages. Many of the preconceived notions of the past, especially those of fear, can be bypassed by approaching labor as a spiritual event. There are many correlations that can be made between the spiritual path and the birthing process. If a woman can attune herself to the aspects of childbirth that are wondrous, then her labor can be, for both mother and child, an ecstatic event that will influence their relationship in a most positive way.

For many sensitive women, pregnancy is a time of great emotional ups and downs and spiritual revelations. Labor is a microcosm of the entire pregnancy process. If a woman has dealt with her changes in a conscious way during pregnancy,

---

Elizabeth Rechtschaffen is a practicing midwife.

then labor will not seem unmanageable. Thus, preparation for labor really starts at the beginning of pregnancy as a woman devotes her attention to finding ways of dealing with the changing emotional tides that rise and fall with greater intensity than before. The following is a list of concrete suggestions that women have found helpful in the preparation for labor:

Find a competent and spiritually-minded doctor, midwife, or skilled person to assist in the labor.

Meditate daily on the essence of the being within you. Choose a name that corresponds to the qualities you feel to be manifesting in your child.

Meditate with other pregnant women.

Become familiar, by reading books designed for the lay-person, with the labor process so that you thoroughly understand the physical aspects of labor.

Attend breath classes with your partner. If you are a single woman and you do not have a midwife or labor coach that you trust to guide you through labor, find a friend who will attend classes with you and be present at the birth.

As much as possible, try to straighten out your feelings with the father concerning the birth of your child.

Get everything ready early for the baby so you can feel free of that responsibility during labor.

There are three stages of labor, each one having its own purpose and corresponding emotions. Before the first stage actually starts, many women experience a period when their senses are heightened and their centers (chakras) open. Some women have said that they communicated with plants and flowers or felt as though they were floating a few feet from the ground.

As the first stage progresses, the uterus begins to pull up on the cervix (opening of the uterus), creating contractions and opening the cervix to allow the baby to travel through the birth canal. Contractions have been described by different people as pains, powerful sensations, rushes, and waves. A woman's reaction to contractions depends mainly on her attitude towards labor. The secret of positivity is revealed during this time. If each contraction is greeted as the necessary force that is opening the way for the baby to be born, then labor will progress faster, with less tension and pain. Instead, if a woman tenses with each contraction, fighting it and wishing that it would go away, then labor will be longer and more painful.

A conscious labor coach can help a woman remember to stay open and alert by breathing with her during contractions. The breath is a powerful tool, used not only during labor, to help one rise above thoughts towards a state of unity with the reality of each moment. Using breath practices during labor can work like a miracle. It makes the difference between a labor controlled by the woman and a woman controlled by the labor. The first stage of labor is the longest. If a woman is relaxed and positive, then this stage can be an opportunity for her to open her heart to the blessings that are descending upon her.

During the second stage of labor the baby is delivered. This is a joyous stage when everyone present experiences the love and purity that an infant brings to earth. Now the energy shifts from the mother to the child as the new being is welcomed to the world. Unfortunately, this event has received little attention in our culture, but we are now beginning to realize the significance of those first breaths taken outside the womb. It is important for women who are interested in a conscious birth process to help the infant make a peaceful entry. This can be done by making the birthing environment quiet and free from bright lights and commotion. It is also important for the infant to be with its mother and father from the beginning to give continuity to the experience the infant has just had during conception and pregnancy. The last stage of labor, the delivery of the placenta, completes the labor.

What happens after birth depends upon a lifelong process of relationship. Yet a woman's first experience with her child during birth can affect her profoundly and set the tone for the role of motherhood. Childbirth is a gift. It allows one to totally open to a force greater than the individual. It can be used as one uses a spiritual retreat. Regarded in this way, a woman can approach labor without fear and with anticipation of a heart-expanding experience.

Love is the Divine Mother's arms; and when those arms are outspread, every soul falls into them.
   [Hazrat Inayat Khan]

Family Life

JALELAH FRALEY

When a loving mother gives up her own desire, for a successful career for instance, to become the first spiritual teacher in her child's life, she manifests the divine quality of self-sacrifice. There are many things the self desires, among them wealth, fame, glory, and praise. To give up these desires for the well-being of another person or, on the greater scale, humanity, is to begin to tread the path of spirituality.

What is spirituality? Is it not finding at-one-ment with the highest aspect of one's being: spirit? And is not the spirit love? And is not love, in the words of Hazrat Inayat Khan: "regarding constantly the pleasure and displeasure of the beloved . . . willing surrender to the will of the possessor of one's heart."

So if a child comes to this earth plane out of the loving union between mother and father, what purer expression of our love for God than to seemingly sacrifice our small desires in order to guide this young life. "Seemingly sacrifice," because the rewards we realize in the final analysis of our deeds prove to be lasting blessings: a poised, healthy, happy, and balanced human being to share with the world. In the reflection of a baby's eyes and in the expression of a small child's face, we see the innocence and simplicity of our own beings, and these qualities are rekindled in us. Then we can turn and face the world to shed this divine purity on a humanity that is thirsting for these qualities.

The loving mother-child couple will awaken in the father deep compassion and strength to guard and protect this beautiful relationship, if he has matured sufficiently to encircle his family with love, rather than feel left out of the circle. There are times when a mother finds she must have the capacity to mother not only her child, but also a jealous father. This is an opportunity to develop understanding and sympathy. Becoming parents can be a maturing process for both mother and father. Together, by communicating their mutual needs and desires, to be heard, to be loved, and to be patient with each other during this growth process, by the alchemy of divine compassion, they will advance on the path.

The child grows older and learns all too soon that there are laws by which to abide. When a law is broken this also breaks the parents' hearts, causing reflection and deep soul-searching on everyone's part. Parents grope for the right words to convey the feelings which come from the heart: "We still love you, no matter what you have done. What you did was your experience to learn from, we shall stand by you. We love you." The child hears and learns wisdom; the parents find the peace that comes with divine insight.

Family life may sometimes include a friend who has no family of his own. The friend learns that life is a process of change and unfoldment and that to be patient means to realize the potential beauty and love in each person regardless of what shows in their personality at the moment. The peace of mind he may have attained as a "loner" now seems more difficult to achieve in the churning of everyday activities. He finds out exactly how much patience and tolerance he actually has in the face of an angry, crying child. And how much real love can he conjure up when someone he was learning to know hurts his feelings in an unguarded moment? The law of reciprocity comes into focus: as you give, so shall you receive. As the thorn is thrust into the side, so comes the opportunity to pull it out and let love flow from the wound.

As the child becomes an adult, he begins to realize the emptiness of the changing things in life and seeks to find that which is changeless. For this he needs a guide. He needs someone who has gone along the spiritual path and knows the pitfalls of strong ego, spiritual power for self gain, "instant" illumination and realization, and "spacing out" with its inability to relate to everyday life. An inspiring teacher is like a lantern reflecting God's light which illuminates life's path. As a fine musical instrument needs tuning by the maestro, so the human heart needs to be tuned by the guide, so that the individual note may harmonize with other notes. The teacher, being the keynote, shows by example how to harmonize with all. Harmony within the family circle is like a pebble dropped into the ocean of life which will cause ripples of peace to reach out to the shores of a restless humanity.

Akhenaten, Nofretete, and their daughters

Love's Spiraling

JALELAH FRALEY

What is this love that I feel? And how do I express it to others? This may well be the question behind the many other questions people ask. We each have a longing to understand love and to channel its divine energy in the purest way. We are swimming in an ocean of love, either flowing with the currents and studying their nature and harmonies, or continually pulled under and tossed about by the waves.

Broken hearts are needed to awaken within us a deeper awareness of the meaning of love, so we must learn the lesson that the breaking is teaching. We must also examine our motives for learning the lesson. It should not be not to feel the pain any longer, or to feel more comfortable, but rather to get more insight, a deeper understanding, and perhaps a little wisdom to help others in our lives who ask this same question out of their own heartache.

Toward a clearer understanding of how to express our love, the words of Hazrat Inayat Khan are a beacon light:

> The angelic soul expresses love through adoration. The jinn soul expresses love through admiration. The human soul expresses love through affection. The animal soul expresses love through passion.

We each embody these four aspects of the soul, and we each at different times may feel drawn to express our love in one or another predominant form. The stages of the love of a child symbolize the different forms of love.

ADORATION

In the presence of a tiny infant, so fresh from the heavens, one senses an angel breathing. The breath seems so subtle, at times imperceptible, like the element of ether turning into air. From the peaceful countenance of the babe love radiates its blessing. No spoken words and no touch convey this love—just the very atmosphere and pervading quietude.

Some grow to adulthood and maintain this angelic state, and wherever they go there is the breath of the heavens. In their presence is the sweet gentleness of love and, like the small baby's, their expression is one of awe and devotion. Glimpses of this euphoric state are felt during deep meditation or in.the presence of holiness.

"The angelic soul expresses love through adoration."

ADMIRATION

The young child with a bouquet of flowers, or a potato print valentine, or the simple statement, "My Dad knows everything," can find so many ways to say, "I love you." The inquisitive, bright eyes and willingness to listen and learn signify love growing out of respect and appreciation.

The ever-developing mind takes on deep impressions, and the mastery of language and creativity fires the jinn soul with appreciation and gratitude for accomplishments. Knowledge, genius, wisdom, and truth are a nourishment for these souls, and from their deep awareness of life, they make love a reality by their own clarity of thought and creative genius. As the fire element is transformed from heat into light, so love kindled by appreciation and admiration becomes realization and illumination. We feel this love in the presence of enlightened beings.

"The jinn soul expresses love through admiration."

AFFECTION

Love finds further expression as the child develops. Smiles work their way around our heart strings and we feel love without question. The tiny hand finds its way into ours, soft lips meet ours for a sweet kiss, and we feel a wave of the purest love reach our soul and lift our spirit on high.

People meet on the street and smile; others shake hands and pat each other on the back; some fly into each other's arms and gaze into each other's eyes. All feel happy in each other's presence. This is a very human love, sometimes misinterpreted as ardor, which is really human affection. Most of us have a desire to be listened to, to be needed, to be appreciated and to be touched. This outpouring of love may be likened to water with its capacity to flow and soothe or uplift and refresh. It is accommodating.

"The human soul expresses love through affection."

PASSION

The soul identifies with the body and mind it wears and with the accompanying delights and desires in taste, touch, smell, hearing, and sight. With the awakening of the processes of reproduction come the thrilling impulses of passion. The very depth of our experience of love in matter is filtered through passion. Indeed, it is through this earthly, passionate expression of love that matter is recreated.

Love can spiral upward or downward at this level of expression. Downward goes the spiraling when self-satisfaction and lust are the motives, and if the fruit of this union must be destroyed, there is sadness and pain all around. Upward it turns and towards awakening it soars when two souls attune their wills to the higher Will. This is accomplished by going beyond selfishness and by "regarding constantly the pleasure and displeasure of the beloved" (Hazrat Inayat Khan). The greatest purpose is served and the fruits of this union can be a blessing to humanity.

"The animal soul expresses love through passion."

Ultimately, the soul can realize a love so refined, so purified, so free from self that it is beyond all aspects of passion, affection, admiration, and adoration. The soul fulfills its purpose for being: it becomes love itself.

Friendship

HAYAT ABUZA

You have in your safe-keeping the soul of every person you have ever smiled at. (Pir Vilayat Inayat Khan)

Women can draw inspiration from prayer and meditation and from the lives of the saints, still there is also the need to find examples of inspiring women right among us. The spiritual models of today will not be found by reputation, by self-announcement, or by a lifestyle set apart from the rest. The new age woman on the spiritual path lives in the everyday world, set apart only by her harmonious atmosphere, her winning smile, her sincere heart, and her grace under pressure. She is found wherever the true friend is found among us.

Friendship is inspiring because it implies the possibility of human perfectibility: the ability to rise above petty self-interest and discover the higher qualities of the divine self. To the extent that we allow ourselves to see perfection in others, we will become perfected. Friendship is standing by a person and maintaining a belief in the person no matter what the circumstances. Once we have seen a vision of the highest qualities in a friend, we maintain that vision, even when the friend is unable to live up to the potential we have seen in her.

Hayat Abuza is a medical student in Albany, New York.

> Friendship is believing in a person, despite proof to the contrary. (Pir Vilayat Inayat Khan)

By mirroring back the qualities we see in a friend, we help her to become more herself. By the principle of reciprocity, we will receive to the extent that we give of ourselves in the friendship. But this must never be the motive force, "I'll believe in you, if you'll believe in me." This would be like bartering, and love cannot be held back pending proof of return. So friendship means trusting, not so much because we are sure the trust will be justified, but for the sake of trust itself.

Becoming a friend necessitates the same stages of transformation as any spiritual path or discipline. In fact, friendship is one of the highest meditations, if we only treat it as such. Meditation is a change of vantage point by changing the consciousness, and friendship requires that we make a conscious practice of adopting the other person's point of view and seeing things through her eyes. So the same annihilation of the ego or self-effacement needed to see from a divine or cosmic viewpoint can be practiced by giving up the ego to enter our friend's viewpoint.

> When one comes on the path of love of the Friend, one becomes non-existent. (Hazrat Khwaja Moineddin Chishti)

To practice this kind of friendship involves concentration on a focus outside oneself and contemplation on the highest qualities we have seen in the friend, giving us a meditation we can practice anywhere and anytime. When we try this as an exercise, the first test is merely to break the habit of thinking and talking predominantly of ourselves. By will power, we can eventually turn our interest outward toward others. In fact, one finds that the adepts of this particular meditation cannot easily be drawn into conversation about themselves, because they steer every subject toward other

116

people. When self-interest is denied its usual expression, the consciousness begins to rise in freedom.

After quelling the ego, we must subject our actions and motivations to the test of sincerity. Does our friendship come from deep within so that every part of us genuinely reverberates with our gestures of friendship? The third test is that of constancy: will we sustain this attentiveness to our ideal? Perhaps the real meaning of friendship is revealed to us only in its lapse. When a friend has disappointed us by criticizing without giving the benefit of the doubt, or when a friend has left us heart-broken, the pain of being let down by someone we had counted on causes us to consider carefully our behavior toward those who count on us. With sensitivity increased, we may seem to fall short even more. Learning the art of friendship will take time.

If we contemplate daily on friendship and on our friends, we begin to see that we do not rationally choose our friends. We are drawn to—or thrown in juxtaposition with—people and situations as part of our unfoldment. When we have problems with some aspect of a friend's personality, it often represents a part of our own personality that we do not yet accept. "Remember that some people are bothered by traits in people that we hardly notice, and others are immune to traits we find most aggravating. This illustrates that what we see in another is a projection of ourselves"[1] We should focus on the lesson to be learned about ourselves, rather than think about how the other person ought to change. What quality is life trying to draw out of us by this situation or person? In fact, if we repeatedly find ourselves dealing with the same kind of thorny people, it may be because there is something particular that we have not learned yet. Until we learn, the

---

[1] Pir Vilayat Inayat Khan, *Retreat Manual* (New Lebanon, N.Y.: Sufi Order, 1976), Meditations on Relationships C.4.

situation or person will recur, giving us fresh chances for growth and change.

The goal of friendship is nothing less than total transformation; the opportunities for friendship are present right in all our life situations; the experience of friendship is a true miracle. It is one of those blessings we take for granted, like the sun coming up every day. If it happened only once a year, everyone would come out to watch. Similarly, if we were deprived of the light and warmth of our friends, then we would recognize the treasure we have.

> The man who has proved in his life to be the friend of every person he meets, in the end will prove to be the friend of God. (Hazrat Inayat Khan, *The Complete Sayings*)

If we wish an example of how to live a spiritual life while functioning in the world, we must look to the friend. Friendship is a form of spiritual nurturance that we are all called on to give and to receive in everyday life; it is a balm to the soul. The lessons of give and take learned in friendship will elevate all of humanity to a higher standard. If you have found a true friend, you have come into the presence of God.

MEDITATION EXERCISES FOR FRIENDSHIP

Ask yourself periodically during the day, "What effect am I having on other people? Does contact with me lift their spirits and cause them to flower, or do I lower the mood and drain energy? Are people attracted to me or do they draw away?"

Think of the persons you are attracted to in life who "give you a lift." Contemplate on what it is about them that draws you to them. Realize that their qualities could not stir you so deeply if they did not resonate qualities already present inside yourself. Meditate on these qualities as potentials in you waiting to be expressed.

(This meditation can be practiced both with a friendship under stress and with a friendship enjoying prosperity.)

Meditate on a friend. See the events of your relationship over the passage of time. Identify the impulse that drew you to each other and see the reasons why all that has happened between you happened as it did. See the direction and the purpose it has all been working toward. See the qualities in yourself that required the crucible of this relationship to be revealed and affirmed.

See the relationship as it is now. Sense the direction it will be called to move in the future. See how every part of the past was leading exactly to this present opportunity. Become aware of any blockages created by problems, grudges, hurt feelings, or any other unspoken feelings that need to be brought out into the open.

Identify what change or quality in yourself will be needed to meet this challenge. Do not expect the other person or the situation itself to change, but what could you change in yourself that would make what seemed to be an obstacle in your friendship no longer an obstacle?

Do you need to let go of an expectation? Do you need the courage to talk about a matter that seems too frightening to bring up? Can you resist the temptation to try to make your friend over in your own image?

Now finally, see yourself taking this next step in the relationship. Imagine yourself able to achieve or embody the next stage of friendship.

THREE EXERCISES WE CAN USE TO
OVERCOME DIFFICULTIES WITH FRIENDS

Recognize the natural habit of your egocentric mind to favor its own rationales, and by will power discount them several-fold, giving extra weight in your mind to the possible excuses and reasons for your friend's actions which disturb you.

Ask yourself: when things go poorly, do you get discouraged and think that the relationship will always be that way? Then when things go well, do you fearfully assume that the success will be short-lived? Concentrate on believing the reverse.

Never talk about a friend. This jeopardizes your future interactions, because talking about a person, especially criticizing a person, leaves a negative residue, even if your friend never knows. It also cheapens you in the eyes of the one you are telling, though some people may encourage you. So stifle the impulse and exercise restraint. This will be very difficult at first and you may be surprised to find what a large proportion of your social intercourse consists of discussing other people. Find ways of feeling close to people other than validating each other's opinions about persons not present.

As a start, commit yourself to do this for one day or one week at a time. If you live with a partner or a group of people, or if you have a regular meditation group, consider making this commitment as a vow together. Experience the rising sense of exaltation that comes from committing yourself to treat every being as a sacred trust. This is meditation in action.

121

Women in the World

*One woman's personal account of how to balance
the feminine nature with work in the world*

SAPHIRA BARBARA LINDEN

To fulfill our purpose as conscious women in the new
age, there are many forms around which our lives can be
sculpted to receive intuition and inspiration and to express
them meaningfully. Traditionally, nurturing our partners and
children with love as wives and mothers was the most obvious
way to fulfill our "womanhood." The woman's role has been
deeply questioned throughout the growth of the woman's
movement, which has certainly been a successful vehicle for
expressing dissatisfaction and making a wider population
conscious of the issues. It has also served to help women
become a support system for each other in this exploration.
Women have helped each other feel less bound by their
conditioning and more confident about making important
lifestyle choices.

But, beyond the external roles, the question that is
touching many women today is how to fulfill one's inner life

*Saphira Linden is artistic director of Omega Company Theater
Workshop in Boston.*

and realize one's female essence through *whatever* outer roles
or lifestyles one chooses.

> There is no line of work or study which woman in the west
> does not undertake and does not accomplish as well as man.
> Even in social and political activities, in religion, in spiritual
> ideas she indeed excels man. The charitable organizations
> existing in different parts of the west are mostly supported by
> the women, and I see as clear as daylight that the hour is coming
> when woman will lead humanity to a higher evolution.
> (Hazrat Inayat Khan, unpublished writings)

The process of working toward an awakening of
consciousness in humanity through our careers necessitates
a deep understanding of the richness of our female essence.
There is the High Priestess or receptive part which listens,
hears, and receives the inner guidance or inspiration. There
is also the Empress or expressive part which brings inspiration
into creative manifestation in the world. These two forces must
work in balance. Some of us are initially more attuned to one
or the other, but it is encouraging to know that we are each
capable of developing the other. As new age women, we are
learning how to balance the receptive and expressive aspects.
When one is off balance internally, then everything reflects
that imbalance externally.

All of us are given different kinds of relationships and
life situations within which to learn that balance, learn our
life lessons, unfold our qualities, and fulfill our life purpose.
For some of us, the major "schoolroom" as an adult may be
our family setting, for others our friendships, and for still
others our work situations.

> The seeking of every soul in this world is different, distinct and
> peculiar to himself; and each can best attain the object of his
> search in God. (Hazrat Inayat Khan)

In my own experience, my work worlds have been the most
consistent source of lessons and growth. I entered a highly

competetive field in a generally male-dominated occupation of theater director. I was always strongly motivated and challenged to do whatever it took to create theater and the organization needed to sustain it. It was intoxicating to "make it."

I can now see that so much of the excitement, activity, achievement, and outward expression of creative energy came from a natural attunement to the Empress qualities. Immediately after graduate school, I found myself with two full time and two part time jobs simultaneously. So much of this was tied up in a drive for personal attainment and a need to prove myself in the work-career world. I was teaching emotionally disturbed and retarded adolescents at Boston State Hospital, teaching voice and diction at a charm school affiliated with a modeling agency, becoming a group leader for a religious youth group, and starting an experimental theater dedicated to creating original plays and guiding preliminary workshops. I found myself using these seemingly different job situations as laboratories to experiment with theater and its applications.

One cycle led to another. There were some fine plays created, new theater techniques developed for actors and teachers, and awards and critical acclaim. This produced new funding and new opportunities to create experimental works which generated a rhythm that built and perpetuated itself. It was innocent and enthusiastic at first, but as the waves got larger, it became so easy to lose touch with the original inspiration of creating a new kind of theater. The balance was lost.

For those of us who are working women in the world, the momentum of activity can carry us further and further along while we forget the importance of staying conscious and maintaining stillness and receptivity to deeper guidance in the midst of activity. If our only goal is to achieve results and we disregard the means to achieve them, then we forget about sensitivity to other people. Our ideal or original intention becomes distorted.

It is so easy, as I have often experienced, to be thrown off balance in the midst of ongoing achievement. It can be insidious because outwardly there may be many signs of success—awards, praise, and recognition—yet inwardly one feels empty. In the world, success is measured in terms of concrete achievement, financial gain, or status, often at the price of deeper human values, morality, and ethics. In the quest for outer success, there is the risk of sacrificing the larger purpose that the work is serving for the good of humanity in the greater cosmic design.

One feels an emptiness when one thinks the success or failure is one's own. Only when we realize deep within ourselves that it is God's inspiration that we manifest and that it is God's plan that we have the privilege of carrying out, does personal success or failure take on a different meaning. Only by surrendering one's own will to the divine will, by sincerely asking to be used to carry out the divine intention, and by making one's personal goals one with the Creator's goals can the ultimate satisfaction come.

The key to working in the career world is learning to listen and to be receptive in the midst of activity or expectations and values that may differ from this outlook. This was easier for women to do in times past, as vestal virgins and oracles in temple settings, or even now in protective home environments. But the message of the new age is to bring intuitive consciousness into all aspects of life. The woman of our time is given more strength, inner conviction, and support by her sisters to be in touch on all levels with her real being, without having to continually prove herself or fight so hard. Now that we have learned how to use each other constructively as a support system, we are ready to take the next step— perhaps more difficult, definitely more subtle—to guide humanity through a constant and conscious attunement to the finer vibrations of the universe.

As women, we have a natural ability to draw inspiration out of other people. Much work in the world happens in groups of one kind or another. In leadership positions, as director, manager, teacher, or group leader, we can help people attune to each other and create an atmosphere together which is conducive to receptivity. As a group gains more practice with this, the process will become more refined and the group will receive similar guidance and solutions to problems. If there is an initial idea or vision that you want the group to manifest or carry out, then it is important for everyone to own the idea. This may mean that they forget where the idea originated. It requires egolessness on the leader's part for this to work effectively. When people are asked to serve as channels then their ideas must be honored and used. This process must really be trusted, allowing the guidance to work through other people.

One can also be in a non-leadership role within a work group and influence the level of the attunement of the group. With inner concentration on harmony and seeing the group surrounded by light, it is really possible to change the vibration and create a beautiful atmosphere and finer level of attunement. In order to make a vision become a reality in the world, hard work and discipline are necessary. Sometimes when old forms and conventions are broken down, liberation becomes equated with no form or with a kind of lackadaisical attitude.

The path of freedom leads to the goal of captivity; it is the path of discipline which leads to the goal of liberty. (Hazrat Inayat Khan)

There must be sacrifices. One's personal life must be integrated with one's work goals. A fundamental consideration is one's partner. In my life, many relationships have broken apart because of tension resulting from pulls in different directions. I have found it necessary in a relationship to share ideals in work that is done either independently or together. Both partners should support each other in all of their work; it is important that neither is threatened by the other's success. Because of our conditioning this is often a difficult issue for men. The challenge is to help each other become more of who we are. If a woman's path leads her to a career, then it is vital for her to know that her partner shares her sense of the importance of that path and supports her in the attunement of her goals.

What is important is to create and achieve goals consciously in our work. In each goal, the ideal is to see all parts of the process leading into the result as one flow. Creating a business plan, a political campaign, a health care service, an educational curriculum, a therapeutic approach, a fund-raising strategy, or attaining any goal is like creating a work of art. Waterfalls of inspiration which begin at the same still source all flow into the creation of a beautiful lake.

The inspiration comes first as an image, as a strong impression, as a concept or sometimes directly as an idea. How do you know if it is divinely inspired? Here are some clues from my experience, but of course, there are no formulas:

The inspiration reflects high ideals.

Other people are helped by it in some way.

It is totally captivating; it enters your dreams (asleep and awake).

It is constantly with you; you might see the projection of it in everything and everyone as you walk down the street.

It feels like being in love.

There may be signs in the form of inner sounds ringing in your ears or a throbbing feeling in the heart.

There is an intensity in the experience which takes over your being.

Now, how can you attune to the inspiration while at the same time making sure that the people you work with are inspired, challenged, and fulfilled through the work? You need to concretely give birth, nurture, and sustain an effective organization which is consistent with the original vision. This is the real work. One must deal with the myriad of responsibilities, commitments, and relationships to other organizations. In the theater all of this is necessary to see a simple inspiration become manifest and shared with an audience. But it is also what it takes to fulfill the business plan, the health care service or, in fact, any accomplishment in the world.

In all that we do we must remember the unique capacity of our feminine nature (which we can help men in our society develop) to listen and be receptive and responsive to that deep voice within. If we allow ourselves, as I certainly have, to be pulled into the values created by an essentially male-dominated competitive work world instead of following our own values, then we are not only negating who we are, but we are passing up the opportunity to serve uniquely in the evolution of consciousness on the planet by influencing the underlying value system out of which the fabric of society is woven.

I find that listening for guidance takes different forms. Since I have been working formally with a spiritual teacher and specific meditation practices, I have been able to support the flow of inspired energy more consciously and consistently with specific tools. On a meditation retreat where one works toward stilling the mind and emptying out extraneous thoughts, a clear channel evolves naturally. Before these methods were available to me, I remember getting very concentrated on an ideal which then triggered off some form or method to "bring it down." The mind was passive but stimulated by very strong feeling.

"Tribe," a participatory children's theater piece about Native American tribes, was inspired by a strong desire to create a meaningful, beautiful, and total experience through theater for children. It came from a strong feeling that all the children's theater I had seen spoke down to them and undermined who they were and what they were capable of grasping. This led to another feeling that children were so easily bored by watching things and that it would be so much more interesting and exciting to them if they were totally involved. So a new form of a play evolved that was totally participational. The children were initiated into one of three Indian tribes and experienced, rather than watched, the beauty and richness of tribe life and then experienced what it felt like to be pushed off their land onto a reservation.

Soon after this production a new movement in children's theater evolved in this country and a book came out entitled *Participation Theater for Young Audiences* in which "Tribe" was the prototype. I later learned that similar work had been going on in England at the same time even earlier, even though I had had no exposure to it. This is a good way to test an inspiration: often inventions and new approaches evolve simultaneously in different parts of the world. It is humbling to realize that there is a larger plan and that these vibrations exist in the others.

The inspirations come to those willing to listen and be channels. This can happen on a grand scale with a major new invention or medical discovery, for instance, or on a smaller scale with a new marketing concept, product idea, or type of restaurant. Or it can happen on a day to day basis, as we creatively solve the problems we face as women: how to create

130

living situations that support our needs as working women and how to make our jobs meaningful and never menial. We can view each act, each person we relate to, and each report we write up, as a service we are performing and as an opportunity to reflect an ideal that we cherish.

What a beautiful time to be living—at the dawning of the new age, when everything is being questioned and challenged and when people of all backgrounds, values, and orientations are searching for more meaning in their lives. One has the feeling that significant transformation is happening and will continue to happen. As women we are being asked in our own way to transform the seeds of doubt, fear, and confusion into seeds of hope and into a renewed appreciation for beauty and sensitivity and love.

We can consciously create the world of awakened people that we long to see and experience as a reality on the planet. Each of us can view our work situations and relationships in the world as opportunities to see the inherent divinity in each person. More concretely, we can concentrate on helping others to manifest their unique qualities, the essence of their souls. Just as the pregnant woman can consciously help bring the new soul through the higher planes and guide the infant in manifesting its soul qualities, so too the woman in the world can inspire others to become who they really are by helping them give birth to their true being.

MEDITATION EXERCISES TO USE IN WORK SITUATIONS

CENTERING

If you are working in a fast-paced situation where you feel the outer energy controlling you and throwing you off center, watch your breath. It is an old cliche within spiritual contexts, but it works. The process of focusing your consciousness on your breathing tends to balance your inhalation and exhalation cycles, thereby centering you.

Try meditating five minutes out of every hour. This is difficult to sustain in a work environment, but just working toward this ideal makes a person more conscious of her center and when she is moving away from it. Optional meditations:

To begin, it is useful to breathe out tension, concentrating on different body parts.

Concentrate on an image of a still, peaceful lake and see the reflection of yourself within it.

Empty your mind of thoughts. On the inhalation feel your consciousness rise and on the exhalation extend yourself into the cosmos.

RELATIONSHIPS

Within the OM company's rehearsal process in developing Awakening [*a piece about the awakening/transformation experiences from the actors' own lives*], *we began to explore the different ways in which relationships can be viewed. What emerged was a model of four perspectives—four different ways to view the same interaction. A technique developed whereby the director would prompt the actors to switch in and out of each perspective during improvised scenes. We have since found that this same process can be applied in a variety of settings in the work world, as follows:*

First Perspective: EGOCENTRIC.
> *When two or more people relate from their individual viewpoint. "I see it this way," and "No, I like it this other way."*

Second Perspective: EMPATHY.
> *When each is able to relate to the other from his/her vantage point. "I understand that for you this is difficult." "Well, from where you sit it must really look strange." This is still relating from an individual consciousness.*

Third Perspective: ESSENCE.
> *Relating to people as they really are regardless of their behavior. For instance, in a group of people who feel bombarding, negative, or irritating at best, instead of letting yourself be pulled into that energy, stop and look at each person one by one and concentrate on seeing the*

divine qualities of compassion or light or beauty or ecstasy, behind the behavior.

A good way to practice this is by sitting in your office, for example, and focusing on your boss or other employees you work with. See each one's divine essence or qualities like the divine power that may come out as insensitive aggressiveness or divine order that might be at the core of an overly fastidious or nit-picking attitude.

Finally, try to see that person's problems as your own. See them in yourself, no separation, all coming from the same source and part of the divine Being.

Fourth Perspective: LARGER PURPOSE.

Rising above the interaction you are having or the situation you are witnessing, see the larger reason or purpose for that situation. Sometimes the most difficult and painful experiences are given to us as gifts and as opportunities for new growth and realization.

In a work environment, with people who have a broad range of orientations to spirituality, be aware of the judgments which prevent you from seeing this person's unique path and the larger purpose for his/her different life choices.

UNA

A Play by
Hazrat Inayat Khan

In the play Una, *written in 1923, Hazrat Inayat Khan shows through the metaphor of Una and the statue she creates, the relationship of the soul to God. After one has created the ideal of God in one's own heart, sustaining it with adoration, love, sacrifice, and devotion, the ideal becomes the temple wherein the living God appears. "The God which man makes within himself becomes in the end the door by which he enters the shrine of his innermost being, realizing the real God who is in the heart of man"* [Hazrat Inayat Khan].

The attitude of being passive to the divine action is the feminine principle which all souls must experience in order to find Supreme Union.

Dramatis Personae

UNA
THE STATUE
UNA'S MOTHER
UNA'S FATHER
HELEN
HELEN'S AUNT

KING TUT
FIRST QUEEN
SECOND QUEEN
SULTANA
THE QUEEN OF SHEBA

DANTE
BEATRICE
YUSUF
ZULEIKHA
THE EMPEROR AKBAR
A GREEK PHILOSOPHER
AN AMERICAN INDIAN
A WORKMAN (M. JULES FERRIER)
THE SHAH OF PERSIA
A SNAKE CHARMER
BUTLER
GUESTS

The scene is laid in the United States
Time: The Present

From *The Sufi Message of Hazrat Inayat Khan,* Volume XII.

Scene i. Una's studio.

Enter Una, *who has been long absent.*

Una. It is a breath of joy indeed to be once again in my studio, away from all the turmoil of life. It is a joy which is beyond words. It is a happiness which cannot be found anywhere else. My studio has been neglected for such a long while. I have been occupied with no end of things, busy answering life's unceasing demands. But whenever I find time, my one and only thought is to come here and be myself again. Home has no joy for me, nor do I find happiness anywhere else. No one understands me, and all those whom I know are absorbed in their own lives. Every step I take I am drawn back, and all that I try to hold breaks, for it is rotten; the rock I seek to rest upon crumbles, for it is made of sand. In the world's fair everything I purchase costs more than it is worth, and if I have anything to sell I get nothing for it. By the continual pinpricks that I feel through life, my heart is riddled. O life, you are indeed a puzzle; the only solace I have is in my art.

[*Takes one of her tools in her hand.*]
The sun, the glorious sun, is sending its rays to lift my heart to cheerfulness.

[*Begins to work at the unfinished statue.*]
My statue, how long it is since I have touched you!

[*A knock is heard at the door.*]
Here is someone calling already before I have even begun to work!

[*Opens the door.* Helen *enters.*]

137

Helen. My dear Una, I have been looking everywhere for you! Where have you been all this long time? Were you hiding from your friends? If so, be sure we shall find you in the end. You can't run away and hide from us!

Una. I did not mean to hide. After a long time I just had a moment to come to my studio. I have not even begun to work yet.

Helen [*looking at the half-finished statue*]. Is this something that you are working at? Dear me, what a dull occupation! Can't you find anything else to do?

Una [*perplexed and speechless*].

Helen [*continues*]. Una, dear, you spend hours at this useless work in this solitary studio. I can't understand how you can do it!

Una [*after a moment's pause*]. My dear girl, when have I any time to work? All day I am busy at home. At night I lie awake for hours thinking how to make both ends meet. You know that my parents are no longer able to be responsible for the household? They have both aged very much and it's upon me alone that the care of the house depends. Yet whenever I have a moment I come here and try to find oblivion in doing this work, the only thing I really care for.

Helen. You simple girl, is this the work you live for! I wouldn't give that much [*snapping her fingers*] for work that brings nothing better. It is simply a waste of time! Excuse me for telling you so.

Una. Art seldom brings any material returns. Besides, to expect any would be like offering beauty in the marketplace.

Helen. I can't understand how you can shut yourself up in this solitary place! If I had no one round me to talk to, life would become so monotonous that I should not know what to do with it.

Una. Well I am happy only when I am by myself. I don't want anyone to talk to. Silence is never long enough for me.

Helen. Well, you certainly are a riddle! Now tell me the truth, Una, did you read the *Daily Gossip* this morning?

Una. You know quite well that I don't read the paper. I have too much to do. And besides, I am not particularly interested in sensational stories in the newspaper. They generally say one thing in the morning and quite the opposite in the evening.

Helen. Do you know the rate of exchange today?

Una. Whether money goes up or down does not make much difference in our lives when we live from hand to mouth day by day. Moreover the idea of profiting by the loss of another has always be foreign to my nature.

Helen. Do you know the name of the new mayor who has just been elected?

Una. No, indeed I don't. My dear girl, I live in quite another world from yours.

Helen. You certainly are behind the times. Last night I was at a ball given by Mrs. Wilkins. Everybody in the town who is anybody was present. There was music and dancing all night and great fun. There is a Founder's ball coming off next week, and Auntie is on the committee. She has asked me to help her. Everyone has been asked to come disguised as someone they think they were in their past life. Won't that be amusing?

Una [*smiles*]. . . .

Helen. You will come Una dear, won't you? Though I know that you always avoid social functions. But all the local papers are talking about this. Do come, please.

Una. Society life is for people like you, Helen, not for me.

Helen. Una, I really wish you were not living such a retired life. What is the good of life if you don't live it?

Una. I am not at all interested in society. I prefer the life of an humble artist.

Helen. It seems that no one can change your ideas, Una. I must be going now. I'm sorry to have kept you so long from your work. Now be sure to come to the ball. Au revoir.

[*They kiss. Exit* Helen]

Una. I don't know why people can't leave me alone! They live their own lives; why can't they let me live mine? [*Sighs.*] Well, I suppose that is the way in the world.

[*A knock at the door.*]

Una [*opens the door*]. Father, is that you! Yes I'm here. I had a spare moment, so I thought I would come and try to finish some work I was doing here. [*Leads her father in, holding his arm, and seats him in an armchair.*] Well, Father, what have you come to tell me?

Father. My dear child, you are wanted at home, as your mother is not well. When you are out everything goes wrong. Besides, I have never liked the idea of your being an artist. In our family, as you know very well, we have never had any artists; and there has never been any wish for any of the family to become artists. Our people look upon it quite differently from you. As for myself, I never could imagine you an artist.

Una. Dear Father, those are the old ideas. Now science and art are the great qualifications of the age. And you know, dear Father, I do not do this as a profession; it is my love for art which makes me take it up.

Father. Una, my child, though we have been for some time in straitened circumstances, yet we have always considered our dignity. Your mother is depressed, and very often feels sad to see you so unlike the other girls in our family, who go into society.

Una. Father, my society consists of the little works of art which are round me in this studio. I feel at home here, and every moment while I am working here I am happy.

Father. My dear child, there are many things in the world besides art which are to be sought in order that one may

140

be really happy. If you never see anyone, no one will ever know you. There are many other things in life, if you will seek for them. Art is all very well to amuse oneself with, but it is not everything that one needs in life.

Una [*remains silent. After a moment*]. All I need, Father, is to make you and Mother happy in every way I can. That is the only thing that interests me in life; and if I have any personal interest, it is in my art.

Father. My child, I must go home and look after your mother. She is not at all well. Come as soon as you can.

Una. Yes, Father dear, I will.

[*They kiss, and the* Father *goes out.*]

Una. Never a moment have I to concentrate on my work! How true it is that the world of every soul is different; for the life of one is not the life of another. I wish I could be here and continue my work, but life in the world has so many duties that one cannot ignore them and at the same time live happily. Well, I must hurry, or I shall keep poor Father waiting. My work, when shall I be free to come to you again, especially now that I have to make preparations for this ball?

[*Puts away her tools and leaves for her home.*]

CURTAIN

Scene ii. Mother's bedroom. Mother ill in bed.

Una *enters, embraces her mother.*

Una. Dear Mother, I was sorry to hear that you don't feel well. No sooner had Father left the studio than I hurried to see how you were. As much as I love my art, I do not wish to be away from home, Mother dear, when you are not well.

Mother. Dear girl, with us old people there is always something wrong; one moment we feel well, the next moment we don't. What worries me is to see you going only in one

141

direction. The art to which you are so devoted is to us a foreign word. For you know, however poor we may be in our family, there is no such thing known among us as an artist.

Una. Dear Mother, it is not that I love art in order to become an artist. I don't want to become anything; it is beauty that I love.

Mother. My simple child, beauty is to be seen in nature; you need not go to art in order to see beauty. Besides, as they say: the country is made by God, the town is made by man.

Una. Dear Mother, I have always felt that what is not completed in nature is finished in art by the Masters of all things. The hand of the artist is guided by the eyes unseen.

Mother. But what do you gain by devoting all your time to something in which you don't wish to make your career? You must think of the future, my dear girl!

Una. Mother dear, we all make our future with whatever we do. But it is the future that will tell what we made. Life to me is the making of something; it only depends what we make. We each make something; it is we who make our highest ideal.

Mother. What do you mean by ideal, my dear child? There is no such thing, my darling girl. Ideal is not to be found in this world. You are yet too young, my darling, to know this. When we were young, we thought also of ideals, but alas, in the end we found that it was only a word.

Una. You are right, Mother, there is never an ideal to be found under the sun, if we do not make it. It is we who, out of our own selves, give all that the ideal wants for it to become an ideal. What we make remains; what we are is destroyed. Rumi says in his Masnavi, "Beloved is all in all, the lover only veils Him; Beloved is all that lives, the lover a dead thing." One creates a heart out of a rock; another turns a heart into a rock.

142

Mother. Say simple things, my dear girl. This is all confusing to me; what your mother wants is your welfare, your happiness. This is all we wish for you, I and your father both.

[*Enter* Father]

Father. Are you here, Una? Get ready to go to the ball. Have you forgotten you were invited to go to Mrs. Wilkins' house?

Una. I had quite forgotten, Father. Thank you for reminding me. I'll just go and get ready.

[*She embraces her mother and departs.*]

CURTAIN

Scene iii. Ballroom in Aunt's house.

Aunt, *assisted by* Helen, *receives the guests, who are announced by the names of the characters they have assumed.* Shah of Persia, King Tut, Queen of Sheba, Emperor Akbar, Greek Philosopher, Dante and Beatrice, Yusuf and Zuleikha *arrive and are announced and received by* Aunt *and* Helen.

Enter First Queen of Egypt.

Butler. The Queen of Egypt, consort of King Tut.

[*Enter* Second Queen of Egypt.)

Butler. The Queen of Egypt, consort of King Tut.

First Queen [*to Second Queen*]. You were not the consort of King Tut. I was his consort.

Second Queen. Not at all, it is I who was his consort.

First Queen. Nonsense! You don't know what you are saying.

Helen. Let's ask him which was his Queen. He has just risen from his grave. [*She is seen asking* King Tut.]

King Tut [*looks slowly and carefully at both* Queens. *Scornfully*]. I don't think that either of them has ever been my Queen. [*Turns away.*]

[*Enter* American Indian. Helen *greets him.*]

143

Helen. Were you an American Indian in your past life?

American Indian. No; I don't know what I was in the past, but for the last twenty years I have had an American Indian guide.

Helen. Do you mean a living guide?

American Indian. No, a spirit.

Helen. How did you find a spirit guide?

American Indian. I began by hearing taps at the door for a year before this guide appeared to me, and since then he is always with me.

Helen. How wonderful! And what does he look like?

American Indian [*with importance*]. Just like me!

[*He walks about and is welcomed by all.*]

American Indian [*to First Guest*]. Are you a medium?

First Guest. No.

American Indian [*to Second Guest*]. Are you psychic?

Second Guest. Not yet.

American Indian [*to Aunt*]. Are you a clairvoyant?

Aunt. I don't even know what you mean by clairvoyant.

American Indian. If you want to know you must go to a seance and hear the trumpet medium. [*Continues conversation.*]

Butler. Monsieur Jules Ferrier!

[*Enter* Ferrier, *a workman, looking nervous.*
Aunt *greets him, and introduces him to* Helen.]

Helen. How extraordinary! Among all the kings and queens you come as a plain workman! Were you that in your past life?

Workman. I don't know anything about my past life, and I only know what I was in this one before I joined the Four Hundred.

Helen. And what was that?

Workman. I was a workman.

Helen. But have you always been a workman?

Workman. No, before that I was a barber in England.

Helen. And before that?

Workman. Oh well, before that I was a chimney-sweep.

Helen. You amusing man! But how did you get into society?

Workman. Oh, I made a lot of money in the war, and now I am invited and received everywhere. But, to tell you the truth, I don't like the life. I feel out of place; I feel lonely too, and I should like to marry. Do you know of any nice girl to introduce me to?

Helen. Have you been married before?

Workman [*nodding his head and looking mysterious*]. The past is past; the present is present; it is the future that we look forward to!

Helen. I asked you if you had been married before.

Workman [*impatiently*]. Suppose I had been married twenty times before, what about it just now?

> [*At this moment* Una *is announced. While* Helen *greets her, the* Workman *looks at her with interest.*]

Helen. What a pleasant surprise to see you at last! Are you really here? I can't believe my eyes! But why aren't you dressed? What are you supposed to be?

Una. Myself.

Helen. But what were you in your past life?

Una. Myself.

Helen. Yourself! What do you mean by that?

Una. Self means always self; it cannot be any other.

Helen. You have the queerest ideas, my dear! [*Aside*] What fun it would be to introduce that odd man and this simple girl to each other. I will, presently.

> [*Snake Dance*]

Helen [*to Workman*]. There is a young lady over there whom you would like. I am going to introduce you to her.

Workman [*eagerly*]. Right you are! I am sure I should like her! For among all these kings and queens we're the only two who are dressed simply.

145

[Helen *introduces them to each other.*
The Workman *holds out his hand, but* Una *draws back slightly;
then puts out her hand, but without looking at him.*]

Workman. I'm glad to meet you, Miss.

[Una *remains silent, her eyes cast down.*]

Helen. Now you two must excuse me. I have other things to do.

[*She leaves them. They sit down.*]

Workman. I wonder, Miss, how it happens that among all those
who are here, only you and I are so simply dressed. I suppose
you don't know your past incarnations any more than I do
mine? I am so glad to have found you among all these smart
people.

[Una *still silent, looking down.*]

Workman. Can you dance, Miss? Everyone can but me, it
seems. I should not mind trying if you would be my partner,
for I am sure we would make a good pair.

Una [*as if waking from a dream*]. Dance? I never dance.
[*Aside*] I feel my soul dance when my body is still.

Workman [*to himself*]. She seems to be in the clouds. I'll try
my luck.

[*Enter* Helen]

Helen [*to Una*]. Please come and sing or dance.

Una. Don't ask me to take part in it; I am enjoying looking on.

Helen. But do take part!

Una. The spectators alone know reality.

Helen. Come and do something.

Una. What shall I do?

Helen. If you can't sing, recite something.

Una. Very well. [*She recites.*]

I have loved in life and I have been loved.
I have drunk the bowl of poison from the hands of Love
    as nectar, and have been raised above life's joy and sorrow.
My heart aflame in love set afire every heart that came in touch
    with it.

146

My heart hath been rent and joined again.
My heart hath been broken and made whole again.
My heart hath been wounded and healed again,
A thousand deaths my heart hath died, and, thanks be to Love,
    it liveth yet.
I went through Hell and saw there Love's raging fire, and
    I entered Heaven illuminated with the light of Love.
I wept in love and made all weep with me,
I mourned in love and pierced the hearts of men,
And when my fiery glance fell on the rocks, the rocks burst
    forth as volcanoes.
The whole world sank in the flood caused by my one tear,
With my deep sigh the earth trembled, and when I cried aloud
    the name of my beloved, I shook the throne of God
    in Heaven.
I bowed my head low in humility, and on my knees I begged
    of Love,
"Disclose to me, I pray Thee, O Love, thy secret."
She took me gently by my arms and lifted me above the earth,
    and spoke softly in my ear,
"My dear one, Thou Thyself art Love, art Lover, and Thyself
    art the Beloved whom thou hast adored."

Workman. How nice, Miss! I enjoyed your poetry so much. I
    could not understand what it was all about. What interested
    me was one word. You know what that was, don't you?

Una. No, which?

Workman. "Love," that is all there is to think about. All these
    people here are all interested in the same thing—love.

Una. I do not know it yet. To me it seems a blasphemy to hear
    it on the lips of ordinary people. I don't know a being on
    earth who is an example of this word.

Workman. You are talking of big things. I don't mean that at
    all. What I know about love is to be cheerful and gay. See
    how happy the other people are. Why should not you and I
    be the same?

Una. Gaiety is not my way of being happy. What are these
    pleasures to me?

Workman. You are too serious for me. What's the use of being so melancholy?

Una. If I do not join in the gaiety, it does not mean that I am melancholy. I seek happiness in myself.

Workman. But I want you to seek it in me. For you know how I feel when I look at you. You are trying to hold me off by talking so brilliantly, but you look so beautiful when you are sad that I feel like kneeling at your feet. But you know that the thing I want most in the world is to see you laughing.

Una. You can see many people here laughing. You must enjoy it with them. [*To herself*] Poor man, why does he not look for his gaiety somewhere else? [*Turns away and leaves him. Walks across stage. Stands still.*] O human nature! It is a continual study to see the different directions that the mind takes. Yet how few there are whom you can really call human beings. Alone at home, alone in the society of others—I suppose to be alone is my lot. And it never wearies me. Life in the world is most interesting to me, but solitude away from the world is the longing of my soul.

[*Minuet.*]

CURTAIN

Scene iv. Una's studio.

Una [*addressing the statue*]. Beloved image, the ideal of my soul, thou hast been conceived in my soul and I have nursed thee with my tears, until thou hast manifested to my vision. When thou art before me, my Beloved, I rise upon wings and my burden becomes light, but when my little self rises before mine eyes I drop to earth and all its weight falls upon me. Did I make sacrifices for thee? No. Thou art the outcome of my love. How long, how long shall I wait to hear a word from thee? Whether here or elsewhere I have worked for thee and thought of thee alone. Dear, dear image, thou art the ideal of my heart. O speak to me! My heart impatiently awaits thy word, deaf to all that comes from without. O thou who are enshrined in my heart, speak to me! I have yearned to hear thy voice if it were but once.

Statue. Yes, I speak, but I speak only when thou art silent.

Una. Thy whisper to the ears of my heart moves my soul to ecstasy. The waves of joy which rise out of my heart form a net in which thy living word may swing.

Statue. Thou hast found thy happiness in working in this place which is my world. Thou did first imagine my existence, as I lived in thy imagination; now thy imagination has become a reality and my existence has become truth. So thou madest me to be the masterpiece of thine art. Now I am the result of thine art, and in finishing me thou fulfillest the purpose of thy life. Dost thou love me? Then first learn what love means. Love means sacrifice, one continual sacrifice from the beginning to the end. I come to life only when thou becomest dead.

Una. I would willingly die a thousand deaths if by dying I could gain thy beloved presence. If it were a cup of poison thy beloved hand offered, I would prefer that poison to the bowl of nectar. I value the dust under thy feet, my precious one, most of all treasures the earth holds. If my head could touch the earth of thy dwelling place, I would proudly refuse Khusrau's crown. I would sacrifice all the pleasures the earth can offer me, if I could only retain the pain I have in my feeling heart.

Statue [*holds out a bowl*]. I offer thee this cup of poison. Take it if thou wilt.

[Una *takes the cup. Falls down as though dead.*]

Statue [*raises her in his arms, embraces her and kisses her, and brings her to life again*]. Awake! Awake! [*She opens her eyes.*] Thou hast gone through death, but hast not died. The sacrifice thou madest did not after all rob thee of thy life. It has only raised thee above death. Now thou art living with my life. It is thy love which hath given thee the life after death, a life to live forever.

Una. Thy light hath illuminated the dark chambers of my mind. Thy love is rooted in the depth of my heart. Thine own eyes are the light of my soul. Thy power worketh behind my action. Thy peace alone is my life's repose. Thy will is behind my every impulse. Thy voice is audible in the words I speak. Thine own image is my countenance. My body is but a cover over the soul. My life is thy very breath, my Beloved, and my self is thine own being.

CURTAIN

Beauty

ELIZABETH RECHTSCHAFFEN

Into the dark night of my yearning
Came beauty with her burning grace.
And I so blind [and she so humble]
Did not recognize God's face.

"'Tis God I seek," I told her plainly.
"And I, my friend, do bring His love."
"But I am searching for His glory."
"Alas, I only bring His love."

Then beauty kneeled and dropped her veil,
And looked into my eyes.
Her glance revealed the mystery.
"Then tell me of His love!" I cried.

Her tale was like a timeless flame
That set my heart aglow.
With gratitude I bent my head.
There was nothing left to know.

When beauty rose and turned to leave,
I called to her with soul-felt pain,
"Where shall I look if I should lose thee?"
And then, my friend, she said your name.